REVOLUTIONARY
WITCHCRAFT

★ A GUIDE TO MAGICAL ACTIVISM ★

SARAH LYONS

RUNNING PRESS

PHILADELPHIA

To my parents, thank you for letting me be weird.

Running Press
Hachette Book Group
1290 Avenue of the Americas, New York, NY 10104
www.runningpress.com
@Running_Press

Printed in China

First Edition: November 2019

Published by Running Press, an imprint of Perseus Books, LLC, a subsidiary of Hachette Book
Group, Inc. The Running Press name and logo is a trademark of the Hachette Book Group.

The Hachette Speakers Bureau provides a wide range of authors for speaking events.
To find out more, go to www.hachettespeakersbureau.com or call (866) 376-6591.

The publisher is not responsible for websites (or their content) that are not owned
by the publisher.

Text on the following pages reproduced with permission:
p. 50: Klein, Naomi. *No Is Not Enough*. Chicago: Haymarket Books, 2017. p. 117-18:
The Zapatistas, excerpts from *Zapatista Encuentro: Documents from the 1996 Encounter for
Humanity and Against Neoliberalism*. Copyright © 1998 by The Zapatistas.
Reprinted with the permission of The Permissions Company, LLC on behalf of
Seven Stories Press, www.sevenstories.com.

Print book cover and interior design by Rachel Peckman.

Library of Congress Cataloging-in-Publication Data has been applied for.

ISBNs: 978-0-7624-9573-3 (flexi), 978-0-7624-9572-6 (e-book)

1010

10 9 8 7 6 5 4 3 2 1

CONTENTS

INTRODUCTION

Being an activist means, in part, being actively
engaged with the world around you. It's like making a pact
between yourself and the spirit of the earth, that you're going to
continue fighting for it, and looking at the bad parts of it, even
when that's deeply uncomfortable. Once you realize how messed
up the world is, it's hard to let that go—and man oh man are
things messed up right now!

As an activist myself, I've been all over the place the last
few years, taking stock of what's been going on and advocating
for change. I've marched, organized, and agitated; slept in tents
on the path of pipelines with snipers in the distant hills; been
arrested for civil disobedience on one of the largest bridges
in New York City; and seen tanks rolling down more than one
street—under two different presidential administrations. It's all
given me so many reasons for despair, but also for hope.

Why hope? Because it's been incredibly heartening to see
more and more people get enraged and engaged over the last few
years. There's a building sense, around the world and especially

in the United States, that things just can't go on the way they have been for much longer. Young people, from my generation and the ones below, seem to have an especially keen sense of what's happening and what needs to change. People in general are more politically engaged than they have been in years.

Now, it's been said that there is no such thing as a coincidence. In fact, I'm saying that, right now. (Give me a second while I get my first foot up on this soapbox right here.)

I don't think it's a coincidence at all that witchcraft and the occult are seeing a revival at the same time there are great shifts in our politics. In my humblest opinion, understanding and doing witchcraft the right way mean acknowledging its political dimension. Politics, after all, is about way more than just elections. Politics is about the movement, wielding, and embodiment of power in our world. That may not seem immediately tied to witchcraft, but try replacing the word *power* in that sentence with *energy* and you'll start to get a sense of how much the political is tied in with the magical.

Witchcraft in particular is having a bit of a moment—a fact that is still a little weird to me, since up until very recently being into the occult was a bit like the goth version of being a Revolutionary War reenactor (but hey, I'm not complaining!).

We could go into all sorts of fancy sociological reasons for the revival of witchcraft. I could run the data, pop out some cool charts, and delve into some boring statistics about markets and demographics and on and on. At the end of all that, we might have some good reasons behind why kids these days love the occult so much, but what good would that be for us? Witchcraft is about what you *do* with it, and I say that while there are many reasons, scientific, economic, and spiritual, for the rise of witchcraft, what really matters is what we do with the power of the witch.

And powerful witches are getting involved! Witchcraft is in many ways the earth's immune system kicking in at the last moment and, I don't know if you've heard, but the earth is kind of in trouble right now. Like Peter Grey writes in his *Manifesto of Apocalyptic Witchcraft*: "If the land is poisoned, then witchcraft must respond." So how then do we respond? Welcome to the world of magical activism!

This is a book about magic, politics, and how we can change the world when we blend the two together. If you know lots about witchcraft, but nothing about politics outside a voting booth, this book is for you. If you know loads about politics, but your knowledge of witchcraft begins and ends with Harry Potter, this book is for you, too.

Maybe you bought this book for a cool kid in your family, and you decided to flip through it. Maybe at a certain point you went "By science, this woman's crazy!" It's all good, I get that this much "woo-woo" in a book about activism can make some people uncomfortable, and for good reason! Religion and spirituality combined with politics have hurt a *lot* of people, and so some just choose to say no thank you to the whole thing. I actually don't mind if you're one of those people who is side-eyeing this book right now, but I will make a utilitarian plea to you, just once, before you put it down and walk out of the store to post something angry on social media: Magic, or at least a belief in magic, has been around for pretty much ever, at least if the oldest artifacts of humanity are to be believed. And the way I see it, we can either make a home for these beliefs or face the consequences of leaving all this power and history for our political adversaries.

Or maybe you *are* that cool kid and got really excited when you saw this book! Maybe you've read a bunch about witchcraft, and you know it has *something* to do with feminism, which means it could possibly have *something* to do with activism. You know *something* is wrong with the world, but dang, you just don't know how to make the pieces fit! Well don't worry, this book will hopefully be just the metaphysical duct tape you were looking for to pull it all together for you.

This book is about ways to bring your witchcraft into the revolution against what I'm going to call "The Disenchanted World." To help fight against this great evil, I'll be going through different concepts and ideas pulled from magic, grounding them in political history, and giving you exercises to bring it all into the mix. I've tried to keep these rituals and exercises pretty loosey-goosey, since I think you should be able to add your own pizzazz once you've gotten the hang of them. Having said that, I do expect you to, at some point, really sit down and work through the practices in this book. There's a weird, but common, misconception that witchcraft is radical because it "gets you something for nothing" or doesn't require work. Oh honey, if only! I've been at this game for over a decade, and I've still got work to do. Now, don't let that scare you—these exercises are pretty 101. I'm just saying that even Hogwarts assigns homework.

Now, let's get started.

* * *

CHAPTER 1

A Witch's Place Is in THE STRUGGLE

So why witchcraft and activism? Why not just magic more broadly or a Necronomicon-style book that will summon the Old Ones to reclaim the world? A few reasons.

1. I know witchcraft best. 2. The second option would drive you insane. And 3. Out of all the flavors, traditions, and schools of the occult, I think witchcraft is set up particularly well to take on the problems we face in the world right now. Here is a short, sweet, and incomplete list of why I believe that is:

• Witchcraft requires a living relationship with the land.
• Witchcraft emphasizes femininity.
• Witchcraft comes from a time before capitalism.
• Witchcraft is a magical practice, not a dogmatic religion.
• Witchcraft is weird, wild, and hard to define.
• Witchcraft resists nihilism and alienation.

* * *

DEFINING MAGIC, POLITICS, AND WITCHCRAFT

Before we go any further into the relationship between activism and the occult, it might be good to stop and define just what it is that I'm talking about when I say *magic*, *politics*, and *witchcraft*.

— Magic —

Let's start with magic. There are about a billion ways to describe what magic is. Find two people who have been practicing for years, ask them what they think magic is, and there's a good chance that you'll get two very different answers.

I don't love everything he wrote, but I do like this concise definition of magic from the famous occultist Aleister Crowley: "The art and science of causing change in accordance with the Will." In Crowley's practice, the Will means something akin to concepts like dharma or fate, but his description works pretty well for magic as a whole, no matter the specific practice.

Magic is about realizing that we can change the world, often with just our thoughts. Even trippier than that, magic is about realizing we actually change reality all the time, every day, without noticing it. It's also about recognizing that just as the material world has an effect on us, we in turn have an effect on the material world. Another occult phrase you'll often hear used to describe this concept is "As Above, So Below, As Within, So Without." Essentially, both spiritual beings and things in the material world, like gods, spirits, and the stars, shape us, but we simultaneously shape the world around us through mastery of our inner worlds.

You might be thinking, "But that's too simple. I've already done that!" Yes, you have. We all do magic all the time without realizing it. That's what makes it so cool! When you saw this book, you had a vision of yourself reading it. You may have seen yourself getting pleasure or knowledge from it; maybe you even imagined reading it in the very place you are reading it now. So, to make that vision in your head reality, you bought (or stole, or borrowed) this book. Now you are reading it, in accordance with your vision. See how simple that is?

To recomplicate things, yes, magic is made up of the simple, everyday acts of manifestation we engage in, but it also involves reorganizing your material world to better suit the reality you see in your head. Really good magic essentially hacks the part of your brain that creates and absorbs reality and makes it work for you. Something like the placebo effect is often brought up to dismiss "magical thinking." Basically, it's been proven that if you believe something has power, or that interacting with it will have a specific effect on you, then that result is statistically likely to happen, whether or not it was "supposed" to. "Aha!" the skeptics say, "this proves magic is just all in your head!" Well . . . no, that's actually what we've been saying all along. If anything, things like the placebo effect don't disprove the effectiveness of what we call "magical thinking"; they prove it. What you'll be doing in magic is, in many ways, leveraging the placebo effect on yourself to create the life and circumstances that you want. The power of belief is the power of magic.

This is a hard concept for many people to understand at first. You might think, "Sure, my thoughts have an impact on *me*, but they can't possibly have much impact on the material world around me." That's an easy trap to fall into, but if you stop and reframe things, chances are you'll realize that you're already living in the reality others have magically constructed around you. So let's go through some examples.

I'm going to ask you to do a very hard thing and think of Donald Trump right now. Have you ever noticed how he says fake things, pretty much all the time, but people believe him? And, much more importantly for our purposes, even the people who don't believe him end up living in his constructed reality whether they want to or not. Trump probably isn't a billionaire, but he acts like he is, so people treat him like he is. He also isn't fit to be president of the United States, but he pretended he was capable of holding the position, until one day he really was president. This, my friend, is magic.

Lying to yourself and believing it make you delusional, while lying to others and them believing it form trickery—but doing both simultaneously is magic. Another example is the power (remember this word) that large companies possess. I'm almost certain that you have a Netflix account (or that you are borrowing your friend's), but despite the company being so big and so ubiquitous as of the writing of this book, Netflix still hasn't really made any money. Yes, technically they have ended up with hundreds of millions of dollars in profit at the end of the last few years. But after making that profit they need to spend the money, and borrow more, to spend billions of dollars making content. The same goes for Twitter and Amazon. Wait, what? But they're so important! How can they have never actually made a cent? Because investors speculate they will make money someday—or, in other words, they are willing their profitability into being. Things and corporations and people have power because we believe they do.

Now think about borders for a second. They're fake—literally. Borders are lines drawn on pieces of paper or screens, rather than fixed features on the globe. However, they govern everything about how society works the world over. Stand on one side of the invisible line, and you are a citizen, but step to the other side without the right talisman—or, as the nonmagical might call them, legal documents—and you are a criminal. Even if you move between two states or provinces within the same country, those invisible lines still determine a whole bunch of things you can or can't do, and that's only because we have chosen to believe that borders are real.

Finally, let's go even bigger, conceptually, and think about money. Money is also fake, strictly speaking. I like to call money "belief points" because it's something that only has power because we believe in it. More and more, our money isn't even a physical object, but simply numbers on a screen—and those ones and zeros determine who lives and dies in this world. To really understand the gravity of this, think about how wild it is that you can be a totally good person, with a family and people who love you, and maybe even tons of practical skills, but if you don't have enough numbers on a screen or pieces of colorful paper in your pocket, society determines you are worthless. It's totally nuts! Even if you go back in time to when money was backed up by things like gold and silver, those metals don't really have a ton of value beyond the imagined one we placed on them.

As I hope you can see by now, it's true that your mind has incredible power—but it's not the only thing that does. Something that steams my broccoli when I read books about magic or see new age lectures is how they will often shift all responsibility to the individual. Think of all of the circumstances that are truly outside of your control. Is it my fault that rising sea levels washed my home away? Or that the markets crashed and I lost my job? The truth is, you and your mind have incredible power, but it's just one power among many, all fighting, existing, and supporting one another—which is exactly what politics is.

— Politics —

Pick up any almost any book on magic and you'll read a lot about energy. Energy is the current flowing through all things, both in this world and others. It takes different forms; manifests in different fashions, moods, and flavors; and exists in unique ways in all of us. Lots of people have come up with words to describe this thing we call energy, like *chi*, *prana*, or, if you're a big ole nerd like me, *the Force*.

I don't like the word *energy*. I think it sounds wishy-washy, lame, and like a placeholder that's waiting for the English language to come up with something better. The word I like to use instead is *power*.

Power has a bunch of negative associations surrounding it because we are so used to power being employed in horrible ways. If you have power, surely you must want to control, abuse, and mistreat those with less power than you. It doesn't have to be that way though! Everything in the world has power, and although we may have different powers at different levels, that doesn't mean we have to hurt one another. There is a difference between "power with" and "power over" others.

One of the biggest reasons I like to use the word *power* instead of *energy*, and the reason we'll be using that word in this book, is because politics is about power. If you grew up like I did, you probably sat in class as a young person and took detailed notes as your teacher explained that politics is all about compromise.

Well kid, that teacher lied to you, although not maliciously, because they probably believed what they were saying. The thing is, politics has never been about compromise, and believing it is starts you at a disadvantage when the time for compromises actually does come.

Sure, compromises happen all the time in politics. They're necessary at some points. But the important thing to keep in mind is that the people sitting at that compromise table got there through power, and one or more people are going to have their power taken away or redirected, at least somewhat, by the outcome of the compromise. Here's an example: Every treaty the United States ever made with indigenous peoples was technically a compromise of sorts, but if you actually ask the people who got the short end of those compromises, they'll tell you they were all about the use, abuse, and misuse of power. Similarly, history is full of times when people pooled their collective power to change things for the better. Just like in magic, politics is about feeling the flow of power, finding it in yourself, and combining it with other people's to make something happen.

As with magic, everyone and everything in the political world has power. Finding out who has the power to do what, how much power it will take for things to change, and how to raise the power of a group of people is something both magical people and activists do every day. We'll get more into exactly how to find and direct power in chapter 4, but for now just remember this shorthand version: Magic = Energy = Power = Politics.

— Witchcraft —

One of the questions I'm asked the most often is "Okay, so you're a witch . . . like, what exactly does that mean?"

I joke, but it's honestly one of the hardest questions to answer! Witchcraft isn't as easy to pin down as other magical traditions, since every witch practices their craft a little differently. This individuality and diversity are part of what I love about the craft, but it can make it hard to define exactly what someone means when they call themselves a witch.

Here are a couple things that I think make up witchcraft and set it apart from other forms of magic. Other people might also believe or do these things, but it's the unique combination of them that makes witchcraft special.

To me, *witchcraft* is a verb. It's about what you *do*. That's why the word *craft* is right there in the name!

Witchcraft is a witch + their craft. Half of being a witch is about coming into your own power and learning how it relates to the power of the universe, and the other half is what you actually do with that power.

Witchcraft embraces both the spiritual and the physical—it's got a foot in both worlds. Some magical traditions are all about transcending "reality" and moving beyond the physical. It's a powerful way of living and some great teachers I've known are very much on that train, but it just never appealed to me! When you're doing witchcraft, you're working as much with physical stuff like herbs and rocks as you are with nonphysical stuff like power and spirits.

Because witchcraft is as comfortable with the heavens as it is with the earth, it also makes it, well, earthy! Witches get their power from the landscape around them, even if you live in a concrete jungle instead of a wooden one. We'll get to this more in chapter 5, but if you live in a city and don't see much nature day to day when you're doing witchcraft, you are still working with the power and spirits of the land around you. Witches are born from their landscape.

What's also cool and unique about witchcraft is that it's one of the few parts of the magical world that leans toward the feminine. Now, you can be any gender and do any form of magic, but let's not kid ourselves here: When most people think of other types of magic, whether that's Druidry, Thelema, ritual magic, or grimoire magic, they think of old white dudes in robes. There's nothing wrong with that—some of my best friends are white dudes in robes—but it makes witchcraft stand out, like the one female superhero in the movie poster or the one queer character in the hot new teen drama.

Lastly, and most relevant for this book, witchcraft, in my humblest (but really how humble, I mean I'm writing a whole book on it here) opinion, is inseparable from politics. For most of history, witchcraft has always contested with political power, and we need to understand this history if we're going to use witchcraft for political means.

✳ ✳ ✳

A RADICAL HISTORY
OF WITCHCRAFT

To understand witchcraft's place in the struggle, we have to look at the history of the art and how witchcraft came to be stamped out. You may have read in an old Llewellyn book or seen a post on a Geocities website that is somehow still running in the Year of Our Lord 2019 that witchcraft is a religion. This religion, commonly now known as Wicca, is the surviving arm of an ancient pan-European goddess-worshipping cult that the church violently stamped out with the witch trials.

But, the thing is, none of that is true. Seriously, none of it. Witchcraft refers to the various crafts that witches do (hence the name), and while Wiccans may practice witchcraft and be witches, not all witches are Wiccan and historically most haven't been. Wicca is a fairly new religion, created in the 1950s by an Englishman by the name of Gerald Gardner. There's no historical evidence of any widespread goddess cults in Europe; the witch trials took place long after most traces of paganism had either been eradicated or adopted by the Catholic Church; and pretty much everyone killed during the so-called Burning Times was a Christian anyway.

This might disappoint you to hear—after all it's a great story. Just picture the agents of Diana holding secret meetings in the forest while running from the church and brewing kombucha with other midwives in a big feminist cult. You had better believe I would watch that movie! But of course, history isn't that simple, and this cool story, like so many others we've been told, just doesn't hold water.

The good news is, the truth is far more radical and, in my opinion, much more liberating than a fantasy. The church and state did indeed link up to kill witches and stamp out all traces of a magical worldview, but rather than being an attempt to wipe out paganism, it was a way of ushering in a new economy, paradigm, and means of suppressing the population through control of the female body and the land.

As the world moved from the medieval to the early modern period, a whole bunch of things were changing, particularly in Europe and the Americas. Europe was shifting from an economy based on a feudal system to a capitalistic one. In order to do this, the first thing that had to be tamed was the land itself. Before the early modern era, the land wasn't something that you "owned" like

we can today. Kings and lords had territory that they controlled through force, and peasants often worked the land in a kingdom in exchange for protection, but the land in between and outside the control of a lord or the church was considered unowned wilderness.

This land, known as "the commons," was what we call a "de-commodified" place, or a place where you don't have to pay to do anything. Think long and hard about the last time you were in a place where you weren't expected to pay, in some way or another, for the right to just exist there. Pretty crazy huh? The commons gave people the option of being able to "drop out" of society if it wasn't serving them or they wanted to work on their own farm for their own benefit. It wasn't a perfect life, and the Middle Ages aren't a time I'd particularly want to live in, but it's important to remember just how different things were in the past so we don't fall into the fatalistic trap of thinking things have always been bad in the same way forever. When we look back at the different ways people have lived, we can find more liberating and creative ways to move forward.

In the sixteenth century, something called the enclosure movement began exerting power in England and other parts of Europe. This was a process through which the newly forming states and governments of the continent were appropriating, buying, and dividing up the commons all over the place. Now, wherever you went, you were always on land that someone owned. This essentially put a price tag on everything, including people. Since everyone needed to pay to live anywhere, whether by buying their own land, paying taxes, or renting a space through a property owner or landlord, they had to constantly be working in order to make money. Think of it as the feudalism fire sale: Everything must go!

You can't beat these prices! Plants, animals, and people all stopped having intrinsic or spiritual value and started only being as valuable as they were efficient, especially at making other people money.

"Okay," you say, "this is all interesting, but where are the witches?" Don't you worry—I'm getting to that!

This new worldview and economic order wasn't popular with the general population at first, and it required violence to take root, including shutting down peasant revolts, bringing indigenous people in the Western Hemisphere under European control, and finally, eliminating anyone at home who posed a threat.

It's important to remember that violence like this always begins outside or at the edges of a culture before taking up space in the heart of a society. At the onset of capitalism and the birth of the modern world, the type of violence I'm describing was often first inflicted upon indigenous people in the Americas, where Europeans were seeking further lands to bring under their control. These people just couldn't continue to be considered humans if they were simply going to become cogs in the slave trade. Likewise, the cooperative, sharing, land-based way of life that most of these people knew could not exist within the European economy of commodification and hierarchy, and because of this, it had to be destroyed. Natives in the Americas were accused of unholy pacts with the Devil, eating children, and engaging in sexual acts that most people in Europe found evil. Sound familiar?

When this violence moved past the margins of society and into its heart, we were given the witch trials. As you may already know, during this time it was still primarily those on the "outside" that were targeted. Mostly women, almost exclusively poor, and often disabled or elderly, the victims of the trials represented that which needed to be tamed in order for capitalism to take root. "Witches," that is, healers, those unable to work, *and* those who practiced magic, had to be done away with. Our entire reality was about to change.

If you happen to be a masochist like me, then you would probably love nothing more than reading over the convoluted, hard-to-find witch trial records from this time. However, assuming you don't love the sensation of mentally flogging yourself, I'll keep this part short. Basically, it's very hard to study real witchcraft from the time of the witch trials, which really amped up in the sixteenth and seventeenth centuries, and even harder to research it from earlier times, because most people back then whom we would now consider witches—people who cast spells, talked to spirits, or healed and hexed other people—rarely referred to themselves as such. Like I said earlier, *witch* is a legal and political word used against others. Imagine if in the future most traces of Islam were gone, and we only had the trial records of Islamic terrorists to go by as historians. You'd get a pretty crummy picture of what Islam looked like to the majority of people practicing it, right? That kind of scenario is essentially what we are up against when looking at witchcraft historically. Back then, walking around calling yourself a witch put a literal target on your back, so you just didn't do it. Plus, once you were in court, any testimony you were likely to give was probably just whatever you thought the judges wanted to hear. You try keeping a level head after days and weeks of torture!

What we can tell from the trial records and other historical evidence is that a belief in magic was widespread in Europe. A lot of these beliefs revolved around the fairies or, if that word makes you feel like you are at a ten-year-old's birthday party, land spirits.

Fairies and other spirits were said to dwell in certain hills and were not, under any circumstances, to be messed with. In addition to all the magic surrounding Catholic saints, it was common to also retain folk beliefs around a Queen of Fairy and a King of Fairy, although you might know the latter as the Devil.

The Fairy Queen was so popular an idea that a lot of peasant revolts during the early modern period actually said they swore allegiance to her and claimed to be defending her kingdom. One of the most notable instances of this was the "White Boys" in Ireland. No, I'm not making up that name, and yes, it's okay to giggle.

Some people chose to engage with this magical realm further, through the use of spells, charms, spirit contact, and herbal lore. Most of the time, these individuals were women, referred to as cunning folk, wise people, or other regional names describing the same profession. It's possible this vocation or calling goes back past even pagan times into the ancient, shamanic past, but for now, this is just a theory.

One thing is clear though—this widespread belief in magic was unacceptable to both the newly forming Protestant religions springing up across Europe and the emerging capitalist economy. A world where certain hills cannot be built on because of fairies dwelling inside or where you can't work because of an ill placement of Saturn in the sky is a world that cannot exist alongside one founded on work ethic, profit motive, or endless expansion across finite resources.

Another thing that had to change in order to usher in the capitalistic, modern world was how we viewed and took care of our own bodies. Before the commodification and mechanization of the world, the metaphor doctors and healers would use for the human body was that each was a garden! Every garden is different, and while plants of a certain species generally act in the same way, there's always the chance for diversity. Under this premise, healing was more personalized and holistic, taking into account all aspects of a person, just as you would with a garden. The combination of capitalism, the scientific revolution, and the Protestant Reformation changed this metaphor. Suddenly, your body wasn't a garden anymore, it was a machine.

This change sounds minor, but the stories we tell about how the world works end up making the world work that way! Machines are standardized, and anomalies must be done away with. Parts of a machine are interchangeable and detached from whomever it is "you" are (if you are anything more than just a bunch of parts). In addition, machines are only as good as what they are able to make and produce. This turned things like childbirth, previously seen as a highly individual experience, into the mechanized process we know today. It also altered our perception of those giving birth into baby-making factories, further dehumanizing women and alienating us from our bodies. Or, rather, making womanhood about one specific part of the body and how that part functions (hint: I'm talking about pussy). Plus, since the creation of the workforce is of the utmost interest to the ruling class, under this system, all rights and practices of abortion and birth control were taken out of the hands of women and placed in the hands of the male-controlled state.

Given all of that, is it any wonder the maleficia, or potions, that accused witches brewed were often made of abortive herbs or that accused witches themselves were often the ones in charge of birth in a community? Is it any wonder that the stories so many of us heard when we were young involved witches killing children? Eventually, women would be pushed out of medicine altogether in Europe. The village healers would be killed off or discredited, and schools would shut their doors to the few women they allowed in to begin with.

It is hard to overstate the violence of this time period and just how much blood it took to tame the old world and usher in the new. To be accused of being a witch was as good as a death sentence. In almost every case it meant you were taken from your family and home, held in a cell where sexual abuse was common, tortured into confession, and put before a court where, unless you had a great number of people there to vouch for you, you were sentenced to death. Now, substitute the word *witch* with one of our many modern equivalents like *felon*, *terrorist*, *illegal*, or even *refugee*. People slapped with labels like these are often subjected to horrors not so far removed from those inflicted on the witches of old. This is not to say that modern witches share in this oppression or are targeted to even remotely the same degree as any of the groups I just mentioned. But it reminds us of our legacy as witches and our duty to stand up when the injustices that were enacted on our spiritual ancestors are enacted on others today.

The world is in a tough place right now, and the view from my window says it's going to get darker before the light kicks in. These acts of violence are being felt on the margins of mainstream society now, but due to our rapidly changing climate they will move toward the center of society before long unless we act swiftly. Whenever systems of oppression expand, they will always need new witches to burn to fuel their fire. As witches, we must remember this and stand in solidarity with oppressed people everywhere.

It's a bleak world out there, and I can't tell you that the fight to make it better will be easy, because it won't, but remembering your history can make the path a little clearer. We have all the tools we need to make a world better than that of the feudal or even the modern era, but we need that spark of inspiration to go forward. If you are reading this, it is because the spirit of the witch survived through torture, rape, abuse, and murder to find you and light a fire within your heart. You may not have ancestors of blood who were caught up in the trials, but it does not matter. This ancient calling brought you here, and we are so happy you can join us.

THE POWER OF THE WITCH TODAY

Whew, you made it! Go give yourself a cookie—you earned it!

Alright, so that was then, this is now. Given all this history and all this knowledge of magic, what place is there for witches in the revolution?

When I look across the landscape of witchcraft today, I get this weird, confusing mixture of excitement and disappointment churning in my tummy. All the potential witchcraft has to offer our modern causes excites me, but to be honest, I'm a little disappointed by how it's currently being used.

Imagine you have the power to change and shape reality and you have thousands of years of magical knowledge at your fingertips because of the internet. But right at the time when humanity leans dangerously close to the brink of extinction, you use all that to . . . put pentagrams on knee-high socks? It feels weird, right?

I don't think the commodification of witchcraft is entirely witches' fault. Capitalism is really good at neutralizing a threat through commodifying it. Put a price tag on something and you can own and control it.

Finding your inner power is so important, especially for women, girls, queer people, and people of color, who are told so often to shrink themselves for others. Witchcraft is a tool for accessing that inner power, and it gets me so mad to see all this potential energy directed at purely surface-level aesthetic stuff. Are women really going to have our power reduced down to image once again?

I think not, because we can't afford to. Witchcraft has survived empires, and it will survive this weird time as well.

In fact, if done right, witchcraft actually has the ability to not just survive, but thrive in this current climate where down is up and up is down. Witchcraft loves a liminal space and has traditionally been used by people with no other route to achieve justice. We certainly find ourselves in the first place and need a whole lot of justice done.

Here's my hot take on witchcraft as we move further into the twenty-first century. In magic there is something called "consensus reality" which comprises all the stuff people generally agree is "real." Consensus reality dictates the rules of your life and what is or isn't possible for you to ever experience. For instance, it's consensus reality that gravity pulls things down and that London is located in the United Kingdom. Back in the day, you could also say things like "America is the best country ever" or "Jesus loves me, this I know" were part of consensus reality, but many concepts that used to be agreed on have become fractured, now true to some and fake to others. Why? Because of the internet.

The internet has created a whole new range of possibilities in terms of what is considered reality and what isn't. "The world is round" isn't even consensus anymore! All this chaos can be a little scary, and incredibly weird, but I think we should try to be as optimistic as we can about it all. Things once considered impossible are becoming not just possible, but happening before our eyes. Consensus reality is falling apart—and I for one think that's a great thing. The old world is dying—you can feel it—and a new world that we haven't seen before is being born. This is a very magical time we are living in, where reality is reshaping itself and we have the power to be the ones that give that new reality its next form. This is an age of weirdness. This is an age of witches.

Those who fight to make the new world a good one need the fangs and claws only witchcraft, a magic born of a marriage between the earth and the outcast, can give. It's long overdue that we fight like we have something precious to lose and the power to win. Now is not the time to just take pictures of our altars, but rather to use them. Now is the time for revolution.

* * *

ACT UP and the Power of the Dead

Throughout this book I'm going to give you real-life examples of times when politics and a kind of magic came together to create something positive, new, and transformative. There aren't too many groups of activist witches in the past—and that's where you come in! Take these stories more as an inspiration and a way to illustrate what it is I'm getting at. To start things off we're going to talk about how one group in the 1980s and '90s responded to one of the worst epidemics in history.

I don't really have the space here to cover the entire AIDS crisis. I'm sure you know at least a little bit about it, and yeah, it was bad. Actually, to say it was just bad is probably the biggest understatement possible. Between 1981 and 1991 over ten million people were diagnosed with the virus—over one million in the United States alone—and globally deaths have reached over eight million in this decade. To be diagnosed was as good as a death sentence, since initially there were essentially no medications to treat the disease and as treatment was developed it cost tens of thousands of dollars *a year*.

Gay men, black people (especially black women), and trans women were by far the groups most likely to become infected and die from the disease, but because of stigmas surrounding queerness, sex in general, and racism, treatment came slowly, if at all. Hospitals routinely turned people away who were sick and dying, and some cemeteries even refused to bury someone if they had died of AIDS. Those who made it through the worst part of the crisis often describe it as having lived through a war.

Into this war came a committed and smart group of activists called ACT UP whose early actions and protests created models other groups still follow. ACT UP stands for the AIDS Coalition To Unleash Power (look, it's our new favorite word!). ACT UP was able to tap into the power of rage, anger, and desperation among people suffering through the AIDS crisis and direct that power into accomplishing their goals. In other words, they refused to be blinded by rage and instead allowed themselves to be propelled by rage. ACT UP used tactics of disruption, public theater, and ritual to capture media attention and direct its power to advance the group's goals.

Let's focus on the ritualistic actions of ACT UP. For a group that went head-to-head with religious organizations on more than one occasion, ACT UP understood the political importance of ritual to not only call on the living, but the dead as well.

Here's the deal: AIDS activists, including ACT UP, absolutely had the moral high ground in their fight. When you or your loved one is dying, who wouldn't fight like hell for a cure? On top of that, ACT UP wasn't stupid; they had science, data, and hard facts backing them up about the rate of the disease, potential cures, and how effective things like condoms were at keeping it from spreading. The thing is, large groups of people aren't swayed by facts. This might disappoint you, but if it does, I welcome you to look at the book you're reading and remember we are literally talking about *magic*. Moving on.

Because we live in a world dictated by power, magic, and its movements, people for the most part aren't moved to action by facts, because facts alone are hollow. They matter to build your narrative, but unless you breathe a spirit or a story into them, facts alone are pretty meaningless. Throughout the AIDS crisis, millions of people, including activists, died. This is a fact, but not enough people cared about it. ACT UP knew it had to get moral and emotional power on its side to win, and the only ones that could speak to the real horror of AIDS were the dying and the dead.

One of the most famous actions and public rituals to drive this point home occurred when activists marched down the streets of Washington DC, holding the ashes of their dead loved ones in little boxes and urns. They chanted "Bringing the dead to your door, we won't take it anymore" as they walked and dumped their friends', lovers', and family members' ashes on the lawn of the White House.

Political funerals like this became part of the ACT UP toolbox. Not only did it unleash the grief of survivors, it targeted that grief at a specific person: the president. On top of that, it made the spirits of the dead an ever present force to be reckoned with. By politicizing their own deaths and insisting they be turned into acts of ritual, the power of these activists persisted long after they left this world.

Another example of ACT UP's powerful protest tools can be found in the speech known as "Bury Me Furiously." Bob Rafsky delivered this fiery, moving declaration at the funeral for Mark Fisher. This, right here, shows how political action and magic can be deftly tied together to produce a powerful effect. The text called out in red is my own emphasis.

> Let everyone here know that this is not a political funeral for Mark Fisher—who wouldn't let us burn or bury his courage or his love for us any more than he would let the earth take his body until it was already in flight. He asked for this ceremony—not so we could bury him—but so we could celebrate his undying anger.

This isn't a political funeral for Mark. It's a political funeral for the man who killed him, and so many others, and is slowly killing me: whose name curls my tongue and curdles my breath. George Bush, we believe you'll be defeated tomorrow because we believe there's still justice left in the universe, and some compassion left in the American people. But whether or not you are—here and now—standing by Mark's body, we put this curse on you. Mark's spirit will haunt you until the end of your days. So that, in the moment of your defeat—you'll remember our defeats, and in the moment of your death—you'll remember our deaths. As for Mark, when the living can no longer speak, the dead may speak for them. **Mark's** voice is here with us, as is the voice of Pericles, who two millennia ago mourned the Athenian soldiers who didn't have to die and in whose death he was complicit, but who had the nobility to say that their memorial was the whole earth. Let the whole earth hear us now: We beg, we pray, we **DEMAND** that this epidemic **END.** Not just so that we may live, but so that Mark's soul may rest in peace at last. In anger and in grief, this fight is not over 'til all of us are safe.

Act up, fight back, fight AIDS.

To my knowledge, there weren't many witches in ACT UP, and I doubt many of the members knew or thought they were doing magic. However, the results speak for themselves, and we can look back now and see pretty clearly that they were working with some powerful magic. Through their confrontational methods, ACT UP was able to reduce the price of AIDS drugs, widen access to care, and help ease the stigma surrounding the disease.

This type of magic usually falls under the umbrella of ancestor work, or working with one's ancestors to bring healing, provide strength, and give you victories in both magic and in life. It's one of the most powerful forms of magic, and that's why I think it will be great for your first exercise in this book.

MAGIC IN ACTION
CONNECTING TO THE ANCESTORS

Most books on magic will start you off with breath work and
meditation, before moving on to spells and rituals. I think it's
important to get the basics down before you try anything too
hard-core (you should probably give vanilla sex a go before
someone hangs you from the ceiling and whips you, right?),
but you can get those steps from any book. Besides, before you
even get to the basics, I think it's smart to have some friends
on the other side backing you up.

We all have ancestors; they're some of the spirit allies
we come preprogrammed with in life. They're the native
apps on our spiritual phones, if you will. Even though they're
ubiquitous, and not "special" like demons out of a fifteenth-
century spellbook, the reason I think it's smart you get in with
your ancestors before doing other magic is that your ancestors
have your back, no matter what. They fought, struggled, and
died so that you could be born, so they have a vested interest in
seeing you succeed.

A lot of people have really good reasons for thinking they
can't do ancestor work or why they don't want to do it at all.
Hey, some of our ancestors were terrible people with views and
ideas we don't agree with!

Lots of people also don't know who their ancestors were
because they were adopted or in many cases (shocking!) due to
political reasons. Genocides, wars, slavery, and colonialism,
just to name a few awful things, can make it impossible for

so many of us to trace our lineage back more than just a few generations. I can only map my Irish family back a couple hundred years. After that, all records stop because the British Empire had all family histories destroyed.

And that, right there, is why I'm putting ancestor work in the first chapter of a book on political magic. All of us come from overlapping histories of oppression that helped create the problems we face today. Some of our ancestors were the oppressed and sometimes they were the oppressor, and either way we have wounded genes that have been passed down through us that we need to heal if we are to fix the world.

That racist uncle you don't want to work with? Well, you don't have to pal around with him or forgive him just because you're related. In fact, what you should do is sit down with him and try to get his spirit to move on, because having it linger around is causing problems for a lot of people. Or how about that great grandmother of yours who was barred from following her dreams because of some sexist, racist assholes? She needs to know that because of her you're following your dreams and her spirit doesn't need to hold on to this pain anymore.

Ancestor work will make your magic better and give you protection while you do the cool stuff I know you're dying to dive into as a witch. However, more importantly, healing our ancestors and their past trauma will heal you and the space you occupy. Think about the spirit of Mark in the speech I quoted a couple of pages ago. How will his spirit ever rest until justice is served? And what pain must he feel and inflict while in that state of unrest? Now imagine whole nations and whole bloodlines wiped clean because of injustice. How can we ever move toward justice if the crimes of the past are still hanging around as ghosts?

Even after reading all this, you might still have no interest in working with your ancestors of blood at this point. That's totally cool for now! Sometimes people need to warm up with different ancestors first, and you can absolutely do that since blood isn't the only thing that makes an ancestor: You also have ancestors of spirit.

This concept may seem a little weird, but we actually engage with it more often than you might think. When people talk glowingly about women or people of color who "paved the way" for them in their path, or about figures like the founding fathers as though they were deities and not just men, or about the legacy of a group of people we are a part of, these are all brushing up against the idea of spiritual ancestors.

Let's say you're a musician who was inspired as a kid by the music of Queen, and to this day, even if you don't listen to them every day, you have a poster of Freddie Mercury hanging by your instruments to inspire you. Or perhaps you're queer, maybe you're HIV positive, and even though you only know a few Queen songs, Freddie Mercury inspired you to come out or gave you the strength to survive, so now you have a "saint" candle with his face on it, in jest but also in seriousness. Even though both people in this scenario aren't related, and even though they certainly aren't related to Freddie Mercury, it doesn't stop him from being an ancestral figure to them. Are you starting to see what I mean?

If you want to get a feel for what ancestor work 101 looks like, let's dive in and make an ancestral altar! (But if you don't, remember your magical practice should feel right for you, so feel free to bounce around in this book and try exercises however you like if this one is still not speaking to you.)

For this exercise, you will need:

℃ A flat surface in your room or home, preferably a shelf or small table that you don't need to put other stuff on

℃ A cup of water

℃ A white candle

And that's really it! If you would like to get fancier and add pictures or items belonging to your relatives or objects you think they may have enjoyed, feel free to do that, but don't feel the need to go wild if you don't want to or can't.

Now let's put that altar to use! Everyone's magic is different, so when you first start doing this exercise, try it out once a week and see how it feels. If you feel like you need more oomph or if you just like spending time with your ancestors, try doing it once a day and see if it feels different.

• Fill the glass with fresh water and stand before your altar. Hold it out with both hands and say aloud the names you are offering it to. If there are too many names to count or you don't know any of them, you can always just say "to all my ancestors, named and unnamed" or add that phrase after you've listed some you want to honor in particular that day.

• As you do this, imagine a warm light flowing from you to the cup. It might help if you imagine the cup empty and it being filled up with light like water. I can't say when you should stop doing this, but trust that you'll know when it "feels right."

- Place the water on your altar, light the candle, and stand for a minute or so with a spirit of gratitude. Maybe you want to list things out loud that you are grateful for that your ancestors taught you or passed on to you. Or maybe you want to leave things undefined and simply send up some thanks. Try both and see which one feels better.

- Blow out the candle when you need to, and go about your day.

Whether you decide to do this simple practice once a day or once a week, try to get more elaborate once a year. Halloween, or Samhain, is the go-to day for honoring your ancestors for many, including myself, but you could also choose a birthday, saint day, or other significant day. Whatever day you choose, put a little more pizzazz into your altar. Maybe pour whiskey instead of water, or leave out some favorite food for those you are honoring. If all else fails, flowers always work like a charm.

* * *

CHAPTER 2

Shaking Off
THE DIRT

I n this book we're going to be talking big and thinking big. I'll be using words and phrases like "world" and "the whole world" and "seriously we have to change the whole world." Why? Because we live in a big world with other people and creatures that all our problems are connected to—seriously. So let's shake off our lethargy and look at those relationships.

A DISENCHANTED WORLD

In order to change the world (or at least this version of it—but more on that later), we first have to check out the space we live in now. You've probably heard of the legion of isms out there making things terrible for, well, practically everyone! There's racism, capitalism, sexism, ableism, gender essentialism, imperialism, and on and on. It can just be too much to list sometimes! Depending on who you are and where you are, one or more of these isms may be making your life worse than others. I'm not going to tell you what problems you should worry about the most because, to paraphrase David Bowie, I'm sure you're quite aware of what you're going through. What I am going to do is give you a framework to see your problems and hopefully get a handle on how they connect to the struggles others are facing. Us vs. them thinking can be perceived as divisive, but when we really start to see the commonality in our struggles, it's possible to realize there are way more of "us" than there are of "them." Examining the different circumstances we're all fighting is not about breaking up or dividing marginalized people. Instead, it's about bringing all the various "us" together against a common foe. Unity like that is not only crucial, but infinitely possible.

Before we dive into how we can come together, though, let's look into the kind of thinking that drags us apart. Do you ever feel like nothing matters? Like no matter what you do things will stay the same or maybe even get worse? Or maybe you just feel alone, like you want to find a meaningful connection to someone, something, anything, but it's just so dang hard sometimes? It's okay: Lots and lots of people feel this way, and it comes from living in a place we're going to call "The Disenchanted World."

The Disenchanted World is a place of separation—from each other, the land, nature, our bodies, even our stuff (of which there is a lot), and the people and machines that make all of them. It's a place where all the magic is gone, and it's our job as witches to bring it back.

Cynicism, in the Disenchanted World, is often viewed as wisdom. In magic, in an enchanted world, it's the opposite. In a magical worldview, your actions go to where your mind focuses. And it's not just the magically inclined who subscribe to this set of beliefs—ask any race car driver and they'll tell you the same. So why, then, are we all made to feel like nihilism is the best target our minds can lock on to?

This might sound a little tinfoil-hat-y, but I need you to listen to me here. Nothing in this world happens "just 'cause." There is a reason behind everything, from the metaphysical to the bureaucratic. If you feel disconnected and nihilistic, it's because someone wants you to feel that way, most likely because it lets them keep power and a whole lot of money. I didn't say there's a *good* reason behind everything, but a reason there is. Do you think the owner of a company that makes all its clothes in a factory in Bangladesh wants you to feel connected to the women getting slave wages who work there? Of course not! Or what about the company that wants to sell you a gazillion beauty products you don't need? Do you think it wants you to have a healthy connection to your body? And how about all the water we poison, the forests we cut down, and the animals that go extinct every day in the service of making our stuff? Someone with a name and address makes a lot of money for producing those negative consequences, and that someone definitely wants you to keep looking at those things they're creating as just "things."

The gift that witchcraft gives us is the gift of connection—the very thing the Disenchanted World wants to take away. When we do a spell, we are connecting to ourselves and our own power. We can connect to the land, stones, animals, and plants that surround us, along with the spirits we cannot always see, but that are here just like we are. In most group witchcraft rituals, people sit or stand in a circle, often holding hands to collect and raise power. Witchcraft is about connection, and feeling connected is punk as hell.

As you go through your journey, this is something I want you to keep in mind. We aren't just fighting isms left and right, but a worldview that makes the isms possible. We'll talk about this more in chapter 5, but one positive ism I actually like a lot is "animism," or the belief that the world and everything in it is filled with spirits. It's less Beauty and the Beast, where cutlery comes to life and sings to you, and more like looking at the world as a conversation, often between you and your friends. It's the cornerstone of my activism, as well as my witchcraft, because to me it means liking people and thinking that "humanness" isn't just for humans. It's a way to see our world as interconnected on a fundamental level, which is the best kind of antidote against nihilism.

Look, I get it: In a world that's disenchanted, where everything seems pointless and like we're heading for dystopia no matter what, it might be really hard to hear me say you should go out and try to make a world filled with enchantment. Your pain is real, and your hopelessness and alienation are real. Just as real, though, is the person getting paid to make you feel that way, and so are the currents of power that we can change. I can't tell you exactly how to re-enchant the world where you are, but I have some ideas to help you get started.

INITIATION

What is *initiation*? Well, there's a good chance you've experienced it and just didn't know you did! Initiation is any ritual or event that sort of breaks open your brain and makes you realize the world is a lot weirder and bigger than you previously thought. It's a feature in pretty much every magical tradition, since to do this stuff you can't just "know" that magic is real like you know the Arctic is real (for now), even if you've never seen it. You have to know magic is real by experiencing it.

Sometimes, initiation is something that happens to you out of the blue. Maybe you've had a near-death experience, or maybe you've had dead loved ones return to you in your sleep. You could have been abducted by fairies, seen a ghost, encountered an alien, realized you're gay, realized you're trans, found out who your birth parents are, left home for the first time, or had some other profound thing happen that sparked your belief in the magic around you. Whatever it is that constituted your initiation, you probably knew it when it happened. It's that "Oh shit!" moment when you realize you just can't view the world the same way you did before.

Maybe none of these things have happened to you, or maybe they did and they weren't that big of a deal (even the fairy thing). If that's you, just know plenty of people don't get initiated by a spontaneous event—that's why there are millions of rituals designed to create this effect in you and open you up to a bigger reality. Having your confirmation or bar/bat mitzvah would be common religious initiations, and even the first year of college can be an initiation for some! Initiation is not about the motions or about who does it and when. To get really sappy for a minute, being initiated is like falling in love. You just know it when it happens—and it's big, scary, amazing, and life-changing.

With that in mind, think again on whether you've experienced an initiation of sorts. Try to think of the first time you realized the world is really, really messed up. Not just messed up, but full of big, complicated reasons for the awfulness that groups suffer every day. Now think about what helped you realize this. Was it a documentary, a book, or a trip to a different city or country? Maybe you grew up knowing in the back of your mind that something wasn't right, but it wasn't until someone explained it to you that you could put words to it? People like to call this understanding "wokeness" or "becoming woke," and I really like that we collectively seemed to land on this word, because initiation is waking up to the world and becoming woke is becoming initiated.

I remember the first time I saw an armored vehicle. It was late 2016 and I had just arrived at the Oceti Sakowin camp on the Standing Rock Reservation with two indigenous activists who had been kind enough to invite me along to help. I had been following news of the Dakota Access Pipeline and the resistance to it for months. I read everything I could on the camp and the history of the people fighting the pipeline project. I read books and blogs and watched video after video on indigenous politics and resistance, and while that gave me a good baseline, I still wasn't prepared for what I experienced.

At the end of the day, even though I had a lot of knowledge, it didn't mean I *knew* what any of the blogs and videos had been talking about, because I hadn't seen and experienced it with my own eyes and body. On top of that, I don't know if you've looked at my author photo for this book, but I'm pretty white. I grew up in a well-off family in a town where people didn't lock their doors and everyone in every position of power looked sort of like me. I knew, intellectually, that people all over the world had to fight and die for their right just to exist. I knew, intellectually, that racism was real—and being a woman I had some inherent empathy for that—but I didn't really get it until that day.

The camp was a picture of love. Despite the well-below-freezing temperatures of the North Dakota winter, people were smiling, sometimes dancing, and there was an overwhelming sense that everyone truly cared for one another. Then, you looked up, and there were drones, snipers, armored cars, and tanks and all of them were looking right at you, and you knew in that moment that history books had lied to you and the West was never really "won." It's ridiculous! It was absolute absurdity that all this was allowed when all people were peacefully asking for is clean drinking water and the right to not have their land infringed upon. But, there it was. I knew in my head that things were bad, but until that day I didn't feel in my body or heart the layers of oppression, state control, and, to be frank, evil, that so many of us live under.

I'll talk more about Standing Rock later, but for now, I just want you to consider that as an example of what an initiation or awakening can look and feel like.

Now, here's the thing about initiation: It can really, *really* suck. No one wants to admit that they were wrong, and waking up to find the world entirely different from the way you imagined it to be is beyond scary. A lot of people face moments of initiation in their lives and just run.

While this is a totally understandable approach, I don't really recommend it. Initiation can feel like the Tower card in tarot—big and cataclysmic, like your world is falling apart. But after the Tower comes the Star, the sign of newfound hope and optimism.

Put another, less dramatic way, while you were growing up you undoubtedly outgrew lots of things, from shoes and clothes to ideas about how the world works. It may have been hard to let go of some of those things, but imagine how much harder it would be to be a grown-ass adult who stuffs their feet into Pokémon shoes that are too small and genuinely sends letters to Santa every December?

It's important to lean into initiation and let yourself be changed by it. Remember, the world isn't actually different—all the same stuff is still there—you are just seeing it differently, and in magic, perception is half the battle.

It's also important to remember that being initiated isn't the end of your journey, it's the beginning. You don't know everything; you just know more than you did before. So don't beat yourself up when there are things you still don't. (Spoiler: there always will be.) And coming from that spirit of connectedness and generosity we discussed earlier, try not to beat up others who may not be where you are but are honestly trying to get there. We are all at different stages in our spiritual growth.

* * *

THE POWER OF WORDS

In the Bible, what's one of the first things Adam did? He went around like the very first man-baby that he was and named everything! And this simple action gave him power over the new world. Similarly, there's a story from Egyptian mythology that goes like this: The goddess Isis wanted to gain power over the sun god Ra, so she poisoned him and said she could only cure him if he told her his true name. Eventually, he told her, and once she knew this, she had total control over him to the point where she could make the poison leave Ra's body.

There's a magical lesson here that goes way beyond just the pages of the Bible or the halls of ancient Egypt. It's the idea that words have power, and when you know the true name of something or give something a name, you gain power over that thing.

This understanding of the importance and power of names and words is the job of books written by much smarter people than I am, with all sorts of fancy letters like PhD and MD and BAMF after their names. It's the job of anyone who writes seriously about politics, and it's a deeply magical thing that you can and should be a part of. You have to find and give name to the thing that is oppressing you if you ever want to beat it.

For me, a perfect example of this is the magic of feminist lingo. I remember before I had read anything about feminism, I would have these weird interactions with people, men and women, and would walk away with a bad taste in my mouth. I didn't know why, so I just let myself feel small and uncomfortable without knowing the reason. It wasn't until I was able to name why I felt upset and identify what was wrong with those interactions that I started to gain power and get over some internalized BS. It was an initiation and an act of empowerment all in one. I felt the same way when I discovered socialism. Suddenly I had a framework to describe power and money in the world in a way I didn't before. I could name the things I thought were wrong, instead of vaguely pointing at things like poverty and saying "I don't like it!"

Naming oppression doesn't make it go away, but it gives you the power to fight an actual problem instead of just flailing around boxing with shadows. Like Adam waking up into a new world and naming the things in it, once you "get woke" you'll probably find a bunch of new words too, and just like Isis and Ra, if you want to pull poison from the sun, you have to know what to call it.

✳ ✳ ✳

CLEANSING

Cleansing is the first thing a lot of people try out when they are new to magic. You stumble into your local occult shop and immediately become overwhelmed by all the books, herbs, charms, and symbols you don't recognize. Not wanting to seem dumb, you buy a bundle of sage because you read somewhere that it's a "cleansing" herb and you're pretty sure that's a good thing. Then you scurry out.

Don't worry, we've all been there.

Cleansing is important in spiritual practice, but in the context of this book I want to look at it in a slightly different way. A lot of people treat cleansing like spiritual hand sanitizer, as in when you touch something icky and quickly run home to get rid of the bad vibes. Maybe you had a bad interaction that lingers in your mind, or maybe you came across a bad omen, have been having horrible luck, or had a spell go horribly wrong. Any one of these is a good reason to clean yourself off at the end of the day. Personally, I like to cleanse myself before I do a ritual or spell, and I cleanse most objects I buy and bring home with me.

For this book, though, I want us to briefly step away from thinking of cleansing like taking a shower, where you polish off the dirt but are still the same, beautiful you underneath. Instead, for now, let's think of cleansing like a transformational, dare I say, alchemical process.

Even after you've been initiated or "get woke," you're still going to make mistakes; think, do, and say bad things; and have moments of doubt in your magic. Guess what? That's okay! Your day doesn't end the moment you wake up; in fact, it is just the opposite.

We grow up and live in a world that's constantly telling us terrible things about ourselves and others. Even if our parents were cool as hell and we're surrounded by positive people who want only the best for us, it's inevitable that negativity slips in. The great army of isms is everywhere, and no matter how enlightened we are (or think we are) some of that stuff is going to get stuck in our heads. The point isn't that we're perfect or even that we become perfect. Perfection is a pretty hard thing to define, let alone achieve, and the goal is not arriving at that mythic state anyway but rather that we continue to learn and grow.

Instead of cleansing yourself just to get rid of negativity, I'd like you to think of cleansing as something to do to *transform* negativity. Just as death nourishes new life and power is never wasted in nature, let's not try to simply get rid of the bad, but transform it for good. I'm going to put the actual ritual for this in the appendix of this book (along with a whole bunch of other spells and rites to amplify your practice, see page 127), but for now treat this as a mental exercise. Next time you cleanse yourself, stop and think about how to transform negative things into positive routes of change. If you screw up and do something sexist or racist, stop and think about why you did that and where those thoughts or actions come from, both within you and in the world. Try to heal the place that ism-based action comes from, and promise to do better. We aren't going to make the world better unless we commit to making ourselves better, so dedicating ourselves to transforming our own negative patterns, instead of just acting like they aren't there, is a powerful first step.

✳ ✳ ✳

ON CRYSTALS
AND CAPITALISM

This section might come across as odd to seasoned readers of witchcraft 101 books. A witch who doesn't love crystals? Preposterous!

Crystals are a part of a lot of people's magical practice, and I know some people who really love them and get a lot of good magic out of them. Heck, I own crystals! Looking around my room right now I see at least six. This little aside isn't me saying to throw your crystals away—in fact, it's actually not about crystals at all! It's more about what crystals represent in the current magical landscape and how we can hopefully move past it for a more authentic and holistic future.

Deep, transformative change is hard, so hard that most people avoid it at all costs. Think about your friend who just can't stop dating the wrong people. The individuals they date change, supposedly, but each relationship seems to follow the same patterns and your friend keeps getting hurt in the same way. Or think about election cycles, in which the politician changes, but things seem to stay the same or even get worse. If you aren't willing to hunker down and address some underlying problems, cosmetic, surface-level changes do very little good.

I see this happening a lot with magic now that it's going mainstream. People come to witchcraft wanting it to change their lives, but don't go through the work of looking at how they think about the world. With a tool like crystals—or herbs or candles—I see a lot of people buying and selling them like they are buying and selling feelings. I want to feel love, so I'll buy a pink rock; I want to feel safe, so I'll buy a black rock; I want to feel calm, so I'll buy a clear rock. When it doesn't work, the only logical conclusion—or so you're led to believe—is that there must be something really wrong with you or maybe magic isn't real after all!

It's not the crystal, and it's for sure not you. It's all based on manufactured insecurities—buying and selling feelings, especially to women, is just marketing 101—which are based on fears, and when you are afraid, you are easy to control. But witchcraft cannot be controlled.

Part of this commodity-based cycle comes from the way shopping itself is a ritual in our culture. All our biggest holidays revolve around shopping and the acquisition of objects. And it's true that sometimes a financial investment can make you more incentivized to actually do the thing you're trying to buy. But if the number of unused sports bras in my dresser is any indication, you can't always buy your way into moods, motivation, or magic.

Another uncomfortable truth is that much of the "magical" stuff being sold by big companies has been made in factories or dug up from mines that don't treat their workers or the earth very nicely. I know, I know, there's no truly ethical way to consume under capitalism (I've seen the meme), but it does sometimes feel ironic that people buy something to make them feel empowered, when the person who made it is so disempowered themselves.

I'm anti-capitalist (I don't know if you could tell), but I'm not anti-stuff. Far from it! As a witch, I see the world and all the stuff in it as being filled with spirits. I love things. I like having lots of things. More than that, I like to have a relationship with things. The raw quartz I have on my altar may not be as pretty as the one in the store, but I know where it came from, down to the name of the mountain I picked it up from. That rock is my friend, and the magic we do is powerful because of our relationship.

Alienation is the most oppressive tool of the Disenchanted World. If we are all atomized and alone, without relationships to other people, food, objects, and even our bodies, then how can we fight to change the world? Capitalism gets its power from alienation, while witchcraft gets its power from relationships.

This is a hard conversation to have and one that this book can't tackle all on its own. Crystals are the bedrock (get it?) of so many occult stores, which in the magical world are basically our community centers. I get having to keep the lights on, and hey, we all have to eat. I'm not saying don't buy anything, but I think we can't avoid having a conversation about shifting the paradigm of magic from a consumer-based one to a relationship-based one.

The 2016 Election—Now That's What I Call Initiation!

A night that will live in infamy—or maybe a year, or maybe a couple of years. The 2016 election feels like a force, one that continues to exert its power on our reality. The world felt different on November 8, but of course, nothing had really changed.

I think author and activist Naomi Klein channeled this feeling best in her book *No Is Not Enough*, so I'm just going to go ahead and let her do the talking for a sec:

> Trump is not a rupture at all, but rather the culmination—the logical end point—of a great many dangerous stories our culture has been telling for a very long time. That greed is good. That the market rules. That money is what matters in life. That white men are better than the rest. That the natural world is there for us to pillage. That the vulnerable deserve their fate and the one percent deserve their golden towers. That anything public or commonly held is sinister and not worth protecting. That we are

> surrounded by danger and should only look
> after our own.

Carl Jung had a name for a figure like President Trump,
the Shadow. The Shadow self is the "unlived life" or the
unconfronted truth in every person. Your shadow will haunt
you until you confront it and incorporate its lessons into
your life.

As I see it, Donald Trump is America's shadow. Like Klein
said so well, Trump is the manifestation of every ugly, stupid,
awful, evil thing about our empire, comically exaggerated. The
2016 election was the United States being confronted with its
shadow, and for many people it was also an initiation.

Like all initiatory experiences, you can run from it and
try to pretend it never happened, but that will only slow your
spiritual growth down. Normal is nice, safe, and the time
when there are problems but you don't know about them yet.
Initiation is a break in normalcy, when you have to confront
truth face-to-face, which is not always pretty. Many people
wanted Hillary Clinton to win in 2016, but she didn't. You
can point to a whole host of reasons why that happened from
Russian troll farms to Comey or third-party candidates,
and sure, these things had an impact. But even if none of
those factors were in play—hell, even if Hillary *had* won—the
shadow of American politics would have still been there, ugly,
monstrous, and needing to be confronted. Remember the
power of names we discussed earlier in this chapter. What are
the names of things that allowed this to happen?

The thing is, some people weren't shocked by the 2016 election. Maybe they were a bit surprised, but to millions of people it wasn't news to find out we live in a very sexist, racist, desperate, violent country. There are people whose lives were terrible under Obama, and they remain terrible under Trump; the main difference is just that more of us are looking at them now. We are confronting our dark side. If you didn't know before just how bad it is out there, now you do, and deep down, you know that just making things "normal" again is not only impossible, but deadly.

There are hundreds of lessons to take from the 2016 election cycle, and I'm not going to list what they all are, because I can't tell you what your initiation means to you. If you felt rocked to your core by the election of Trump and you've spent every moment since running from the pain, or if you haven't sat down to think about that moment and what you learned from it, take some time to do that now. If you weren't as deeply shaken by the whole process and to you it didn't feel like a personal initiation, think about it as an initiation for the collective spirit of America. Are we learning the right lessons? Are we allowing ourselves to be positively transformed?

There will be a day when Trump is no longer president (perhaps, as you're reading this, that day has already come to pass). There will be a day when he no longer exists! You can do absolutely nothing and those things will still happen, but the shadow may remain. It's not enough to just want to go back to the world before the 2016 election and repeat a pattern of cosmetic rather than deep political change. And it's never healthy to lose yourself in fantasy or anxiety and forget the real world. We need to think about what we want the world to look like as we move forward. We need to dream bigger.

MAGIC IN ACTION
A RITE OF INITIATION

So maybe after reading this chapter you're feeling left out because you've never really been initiated. Well then, there's no time like the present.

Like I said earlier, there are literally endless ways to become initiated. So long as you set into place a shift in consciousness that has ripple effects throughout your life, you've done it! Easy, right?

An at-home initiation should involve doing something a little naughty or frowned upon in society. You may want to read the Lord's Prayer backward or break a crucifix, if you want to go the heavy metal route. I personally think a great component to an initiation ritual could be burning a dollar bill, but my editor told me that's illegal so I can't *technically* suggest you do it.

I'm going to give you an initiation ritual here, but know that if it does not feel right to you there are hundreds of other options available online and in other books. If this one isn't for you, feel free to find another or make one of your own!

While they vary culture to culture, most initiation rituals include the following:

• The breaking of a taboo
• An oath or promise
• Meditation on the personal meaning of the ritual in the days leading up to it

Here is a ritual containing all these components that I developed just for you!

For this you will need:

☾ Paper
☾ Scissors
☾ A pen
☾ Tape
☾ An object or symbol that represents something that oppresses you or makes you "smaller." Feel free to print out or draw an image of it. (You will choose this over the course of the ritual.)
☾ An object or symbol that will represent your liberation. (You will choose this over the course of the ritual.)

Pick a day you want to do your initiation ritual. Ideally, this is a day with a bit of significance. Maybe you want to follow a moon cycle or choose your birthday or a meaningful holiday. Any of these are good options—the idea is simply that this date has meaning to you.

For our example, let's go with the moon cycle. You'll want to start on the new moon, and do your initiation on the full moon. This gives you a nice time frame of about fifteen days around a natural cycle moving from darkness to light.

Once you've got a date picked and the days set between now and then, I want you to:

• Take the paper and cut it into long, rectangular strips, around one inch by four inches. The amount of strips you will ultimately need will depend on the number of things you write down in the next few steps.

• Pick a place and time each day when you can be alone for a few minutes to meditate, for instance every night in front of your altar.

- Every day, spend some time thinking about the many forces, ideas, and things that keep you confined, oppressed, and dominated against your will. Really go to town here, and pour out the things that you know stand between you and your liberation.
- Write these things down on the strips of paper you've cut up. You can keep it to one idea per strip or write multiple things down.
- As you perform these exercises every night, see if you can come up with a symbol that represents all of these negative forces in your life. Is there just one thing or many? What are you going to leave behind?
- At the same time consider if there is a symbol of your liberation you want to give yourself. This could be a physical object you wear, like a ring or a necklace, that acts as a constant reminder, or something you want to hang in your room or home.
- On the day of your initiation, have these two symbols set up in front of you. I recommend representing the symbol of your oppression with an image or word you've printed out onto a piece of paper so that you can easily destroy it.
- Tape the strips of paper you've written on into interlocking loops, making one long chain. Make two bigger loops at the end and tape these around your wrists.
- Once you have this set up, sit for a moment and consider the living metaphor you've created. Feel the weight holding you down. Look at the length of the chains that bind you.
- Begin to chant. I find these words by Assata Shakur to be a

great thing to chant: "It is our duty to fight for our freedom. It is our duty to win. We must love each other and support each other. We have nothing to lose but our chains." But you may choose something different.

- Chant until you feel it reach a fever pitch inside you. When this happens, break your chains and tear them up. Once they are destroyed, take the image of your oppression, and tear that up as well.
- Take the scraps of paper and gather them together. If you can, burn them in a safe, well-ventilated area and collect their ashes. If you can't, just assemble the remaining scraps of paper for the next step.
- Take whatever remnants you have and bury them at a crossroad without looking back. If you live in a city where you can't bury things at a crossroad, you have a few options: Go to a park where you won't be disturbed, throw them away in a trash can on a crosswalk, or throw them into a storm drain by a crosswalk.
- Walk away without looking back.
- When you get back home, put on or hang up the symbol you have chosen as a liberatory one. Claim your liberation.

Write down how this ritual made you feel afterward, and keep track of any dreams, omens, or "coincidences" you might experience over the next few days. These are all important signs leading you on your magical journey.

* * *

CHAPTER 3

Dream Big

There are forces in this world that seek to dominate us against our will. These forces wish to control how we dress, how we look, if we live or die, who we love, how we love them, and if we are allowed to feel love at all. Living in the Disenchanted World can make magic seem impossible and our sphere of influence small.

You may be physically and financially restricted in a thousand different ways, but one thing I hope you never let get shrunk down or confined is your imagination. Our ability to dream a different world is the foundation of magic, and quite frankly, it's the only hope we have.

In the first issue of Neil Gaiman's *The Sandman* series, a bunch of occultists capture Morpheus, the god of dreams, and keep him from the world for years. Without dreams, progress halts, people stop asking for more out of life, and many fall into sad years of dreamless sleep. Looking at the news, it can sometimes feel like someone has captured dreams in our world too. We've got big problems, but our imaginations seem just a bit too small to solve them. A carbon tax to fight the death of the world? A clever sign at a protest to keep people from dying? Small steps can be necessary to reach our goals, but sometimes we are sold small steps to keep us from imagining bigger ones. Besides, even if our steps must sometimes be incremental, why can't our dreams be big?

Dreams are very important in witchcraft. In dreams we enter other worlds, other states of consciousness, and can talk to the living, the dead, and maybe even things that never lived or died. As an activist, you are going to encounter so many people telling you to be more "reasonable" or that your ideas aren't "realistic." Sometimes this comes from a place of bad faith, and the person telling you all this wouldn't want to see your demands met, even if they "reasonably" could be! But, sometimes, you'll hear the same kind of limited thinking from people who genuinely would like to see your dreams become a reality, but have had their own imaginations so damaged by the Disenchanted World that they honestly can't imagine a better way of being. They've forgotten, or maybe never realized, that dreams and reality have a lot more overlap than we like to think. As witches, it's important to remember that.

Look around you, and recognize that everything you see was once immaterial, a dream in someone's head. The chair you're sitting on, the lamp you're reading with, the book you have in your hands right now—all this once existed as nothing more than a thought. Then, someone, or a bunch of people, decided to use their power to make the immaterial, material. They did magic through this altering of reality, and even if all they did was make a new chair, they changed the world. The art of dreaming—of dreaming big—and pulling things out of the realm of imagination and into this world is what all good magic is about. If we are going to use magic to take on big problems, we can't let our dreams be anything other than massive. So let's relearn how to dream and dream big.

✳ ✳ ✳

JOURNEYING, DREAMING, AND SOUL FLIGHT

Close your eyes and think of a witch. What do you see? Maybe it's a woman with green skin and warts on her nose; maybe there's a black cat; and maybe she's wearing a pointed hat. Whatever your witch looked like, it's very possible she was also flying on a broomstick by the light of the moon.

Flying and witches go together like pineapple on pizza (I've chosen my side in this war). There's a reason witches were long believed to fly, and there's even more reason why witches need to fly now.

Let's get back in the time machine and look at history for a bit. Like a lot of things involved with witchcraft, the reasons behind the iconography of witches flying on broomsticks is #complicated. We know witches flew for many reasons—to get to the sabbath, cure people, make people sick, help or hurt crops, and meet up with other witches in secret. We also know one way a lot of witches were said to fly was by rubbing something called a "flying ointment" all over them. That ointment usually contained herbs that have psychedelic properties, like belladonna, henbane, and mugwort. As for the broom, well, some people think it's a sex thing, while others think it's a tripping out thing. I personally like a modern reading of the broom as a symbol. What better "fuck you" to the patriarchy than to take one of its tools meant to confine you and instead use it to free yourself?

Don't get too excited now, because I'm not about to teach you how to trip balls or literally fly. There's an internet out there for you to figure out the first one (though, of course, I'm once again not suggesting you try anything illegal), and there are planes for the second. As for the few herbs I listed above, please, *please* don't do anything with any of them until you've done your research and know the dangers.

The flying we're talking about, historically and today, isn't about making the human body drift through the air, but instead making the soul or spirit fly away from the body. You may have read other books that give this process names like shamanic journeying, guided meditation, or out-of-body experiences. Maybe you've even done some of these yourself! After you put this book down, feel free to use the term you like best. In this book we're talking witchcraft, so we're going to call it soul flight.

Like initiation, soul flight can occur spontaneously in the form of dreams or on command through meditation and whatever (carefully used) substances you prefer to take or not. Like the witches of old, there's really no limit to what you can use soul flight for! Fly to discover spiritual guides, connect with the land, talk to your ancestors, or figure out how to get out of a tricky situation you may be facing in life.

For this chapter though, we're focusing on flying for two reasons:

1. To teach you to trust your dreams and imagination.
2. To go to places where the answers to our problems can be found and bring that wisdom back here.

There are obviously some important caveats I need to make in this bit. Please, for the love of all the gods, use your best judgment and don't just believe what someone is telling you because they saw it while doing soul flight. I'm writing a book, not starting a cult. Also, be aware that not every being in the realms you can fly to is honest, trustworthy, or quite honestly gives a fuck about you.

Imagine you move somewhere new that you've never even visited before. You'd probably want to explore the neighborhood. Maybe, if you had friends or family in the area (remember those ancestors we talked about on page 28?), you'd ask them what places you should visit or what people they know so you can make new friends. You probably would avoid that creepy alley at night until you knew the neighborhood a bit better, right? And I'm hoping you know it's a bad idea to just walk up to random strangers and ask to be their best friend.

This is what soul flight is like. We have this idea that all spirits and gods have our best interest at heart, but that's like saying all strangers on the subway have your best interest at heart. If something bad happened to you on the subway, certainly some people would help you, while others would remain indifferent, and some might even take advantage of you. As you practice soul flight more and more, you'll find spirits and maybe even gods that want to be your friends and help you out, but don't assume out of the gate that you're going to be Snow White walking through the forest making friends with every creature you pass.

＊ ＊ ＊

OTHER WORLDS ARE POSSIBLE

So, why am I talking to you about spirits and flying in a book about activism? Well, there are a few reasons. First off, before you set about transforming the world, it's probably best if you go out and see the other worlds you want to transform it into.

Witchcraft lives at the crossroads, magically speaking. It's not fully here, but it's not really there either. This can make life difficult sometimes. (Remember when I spent an entire chapter defining what witchcraft is and you were still kind of confused?) But it also gives us witches and mischief-makers a real advantage when it comes to activism. The goal of activism is to change the world into one you think it should be. This is also not coincidently the goal of magic, but in magic we don't have to sit around hoping better worlds are out there—we can go visit them right now!

Look, I understand if you are coming from the world of material, brass tacks politics. If that's the case and this is your first book on magic, this chapter is probably going to be weird to you. Heck, even if you've read some books on witchcraft, this chapter might be weird! We're not used to using our dreams like this or even dreaming this way at all! Plus, even if we don't like the world we find ourselves in, it's still the one we know best, and there's comfort in that. Sidestepping it and taking a look around the neighborhood can be a little jarring. There is also always going to be that nagging voice in your head that tells you none of this "stuff" is "real." Do your best to ignore that. Eventually the results you get from opening yourself up to magic will calm down that worry.

One other big reason to incorporate soul flight into your magical activist practice is to get a better perspective on what it is exactly that you're fighting for and against. It's really easy to get caught up in small battles that make us lose sight of the larger war. I remember there was a particularly bad week where battle after battle seemed to be lost and the world felt like it was just going to keep getting darker. I remember really doubting my activism in that moment, wondering why it was that I was doing the work I was doing if it didn't matter. It wasn't until I sat myself down and let my soul fly away from this world for a bit that I remembered why I was fighting and saw those losses in the context of a bigger struggle, one that I was just one piece of. Over time, soul flight will give you insight and perspective into the nature of reality, transformation, and morality that I personally have found invaluable.

Standing Rock

Our reality is formed by "truths" we take for granted, and these truths are created by power. Whatever your unshakable truths are, they form the basis of what you believe is possible. It was once unthinkable that there could be a society without kings and queens running the show. It was once unthinkable that women could do, well, almost anything, but people dared to dream. More than that, they dared to make their dreams real. They shifted power, and those truths changed and reality along with them.

This is why dreaming impossible dreams is so important. You have to be willing to send your mind to someplace else, someplace better, and bring that knowledge back to this place in order to change it. You then have to live like that reality is already here, breathing it into being with your power and magic. As witches, we have the ability to shape the framework of what is possible and re-enchant the world.

One of the best examples of this comes from the Standing Rock Sioux protests against the Dakota Access Pipeline. Members of the Standing Rock Sioux tribe were given notice that a pipeline was going to be built through their land. The company building it had a terrible history of constructing leaky pipelines, and the tribe knew that if it was built it would almost definitely leak, contaminating their water supply. On top of that, the plans for the pipeline were set to pass near their sacred burial grounds. When a white community north of the tribe asked for the pipeline to be moved away from them, they were listened to, but when the Sioux asked, they were not.

This was the backdrop for an occupation of the land the proposed pipeline was set to be built through. Thousands came from around the world to the Oceti Sakowin and Sacred Stone camps, and the occupation lasted months before its tragic demise.

I've already talked a bit about the bad stuff in this book (see page 40). Dogs were sicced on people, water was sprayed on protesters, sometimes in subzero temperatures, and helicopters from private security forces circled the camp at all times; to say the area surrounding the camp resembled a war zone would be no exaggeration. The brutal opposition to a completely justified and peaceful protest was disgusting and well documented. I urge you to research it when you put this book down.

What I want to talk about now is the positive side of Standing Rock. To say it was a protest downplays the scale and power of that collective action. Standing Rock was an experiment in dreaming, a proof-positive case that another world is possible. In a lot of ways, Standing Rock was the "normal" world flipped on its head. Indigenous people led in all things, and food, medicine, and clothing were all free to those who needed it. Signs around the camp reminded people that as long as they were there, they were engaging in an act of prayer, not protest. Every morning songs were sung around one of the sacred fires, and a procession was led to the Cannonball River, the river we were trying to protect, and prayers offered to it. One woman I met told me a story of how she and other women approached the police line to pray one day. They knelt down in the street, and officers pointed guns in their faces. This woman said she looked up into the officers' faces, and they became so filled with shame they had to look away. She said in that moment she became aware that a power and strength lived within her and that for as long as she lived that power could never be taken away.

The power of Standing Rock came from the indigenous people leading it, because they had no choice but to fight and because they had the cultural knowledge that things don't have to be this way. They knew this, and for almost a year they dreamed that world into a reality.

There are two ways to do a spell. One, you know. In the first method, you pick a goal, get some supplies together, and do something magical like lighting a candle or chanting. The other way is by embodying your spell so that all your actions over an hour, day, year, or lifetime reflect the reality you are creating. Standing Rock is an excellent example of the second kind of spell.

Just to remind you: I'm white—like, really white, like, grew up on Cape Cod white. Because of this, I'm not trying to pretend that I know something the indigenous people who led Standing Rock didn't know. I'm also not telling my fellow whites to copy exactly what people at the camp were doing.

There is a difference between being inspired by something and appropriating it. Yes, I am deeply inspired by the work of indigenous activists, and yes, some of our struggles overlap. The strength of their spirituality, which managed to last through genocides, inspires me to look back at what animistic threads I can pull from my own heritage and add to my magic. Their courage to fight against incredible odds inspires me in my activism, but it's not my job to come in and act like this was my idea the whole time.

You *can* join a fight that's not "for" you. In fact, we should all be fighting for the liberation of people besides ourselves. However, joining a fight doesn't mean you have to, or should, lead it. You can practice magic without pretending you're part of a tradition you aren't a part of, and you can fight for someone else's liberation without making it about you. It's easier than you think! Just like so much of magic, it's about quieting the ego and asking yourself honestly what it is you want to do.

Cultivate humility. There was a time you weren't initiated at all, and there are still truths you haven't been initiated into. Standing Rock, like I already said, was an initiation for me. My magic, my activism, and my self haven't been the same since. I want to pass on its lessons to you, but in order to do that, I have to acknowledge it comes from people with much stronger and older magic than mine.

Never let your dreams be small, or your magic will be small too. It is our job as witches to shift what people think is possible and, in doing so, change reality. We should be less interested in trying to describe how things are and more interested in showing how different things could be.

MAGIC IN ACTION
SHAPE-SHIFTING AND SOUL FLIGHT

Okay, so how do we actually *do* any of the things I've been talking about in this chapter?

Like pretty much everything in this book, there are lots of different ways, but here's one method I've found that works best for me. It's not something that looks particularly exciting or magical on the outside, but I promise it's one of the most rewarding and transformative practices you can engage in. It takes time and repetition—for me it took years to get really good at it—but even if it doesn't come naturally, keep it up! You may find other forms of magic come easier to you, but learning to achieve soul flight is like riding a broom for the first time: you won't ever forget it.

For this, you will need:

☾ . . . nothing!

All you need is you! You'll notice that the exercises I'm teaching you in this book don't require you to buy anything or use much more than stuff you probably already have in your house. That's because for most magic, you don't really have to purchase anything—seriously. If someone ever tells you that you can't do magic without buying something from them, walk away.

For this exercise in particular, what you're basically doing is meditating, so all you'll need is yourself, an hour or so of guaranteed alone time, and a quiet place to sit or lay down.

Beyond that, I personally like to light a stick of incense while engaging in soul flight, both as an offering to my spirits and as a personal timer. I also like to have a steady, slow drumbeat playing in my ears. I recommend putting on head-phones and finding one of the many "shamanic drumming" videos on YouTube to play while you do this. In my experience, having a steady rhythm of some sort going makes it easier to tune out your own thoughts as well as your upstairs neighbors, who will inevitably be moving furniture around. Drumbeats designed for meditation will also usually mark when it's time to pull yourself out of meditation and start to return to earth, which is much less jarring than a timer set on your phone or watch.

Regardless of what extra tools you decide to use or not use, here's my super-bare-bones formula for soul flight. Don't feel bad if you don't get it "right" the first time or even the first few times—it usually takes some practice to get the hang of it. Also, hard as it might be, try not to worry that you're "making all this is up" or that it's just "in your head."

To achieve soul flight, we're going to use a meditative technique called shape-shifting. No, I'm not going to teach you how to turn your body into another body just like that, but I am going to teach you how to do that with your spirit in another world.

Why shape-shifting? Well, one very posh reason is that it's tradition! Witches have been turning into animals to work their magic for years. The famous Scottish witch Isobel Gowdie used to transform herself into a hare in order to get to the sabbath undetected. Her testimony is important to us for two reasons: One: it's metal as hell. And two: she offered up her confession without torture to her witch hunters, making her descriptions of folk magic more believable. During Isobel's testimony, given at her trial in Scotland in 1662, she gives us this chant to transform:

> I shall go into a hare,
> With sorrow and sych and meickle care;
> And I shall go in the Devil's name,
> Ay while I come home again.

And to transform back, she used this one:

> Hare, hare, God send thee care.
> I am in a hare's likeness now,
> But I shall be in a woman's likeness even now.

By the way, feel free to use this as inspiration if you need a little chanting to get you into this headspace.

Hares, bats, toads, wolves, goats, snakes, crows, ravens, cats, and owls were among the most popular animals witches took the form of in order to achieve soul flight and do magic. These were often called a witch's "familiar." You might find one, or more likely a couple, to be very useful and helpful allies to you in your magic. This could be a whole chapter in itself, but I recommend doing some research on familiars and feeling out if any of the creatures either on the list here or elsewhere suit you.

Transforming into an animal gives you other advantages too. Spirits who might want to pick on you may leave you alone if you are disguised as something else.

Once you have a familiar chosen, or at least one you would like to work with, and at minimum an hour of free time, you can begin.

- Find a place to sit or lay down. I like to lay down flat, but sitting on a pillow, maybe in front of your altar, works great too. It's all about what makes you feel most comfortable and able forget you have a body.

- Light any candles or incense you want, and start the drumming record if you are using one. If not, set a timer to go off between a half hour and an hour from when you begin.

- Close your eyes, and start to focus on your breath or the sound of drumming. Your thoughts are going to wander, especially at first. Don't worry, and don't be hard on yourself. Just acknowledge your thoughts, let them pass, and bring your attention back to the present.

- Once you are more or less "in the zone," bring your attention to your body. Visualize it as if you are looking at it from the outside. Slowly, start to feel your bones, how strong and rigid they are to hold your whole body together. Then feel your muscles: Where are they loose? Where are they sore? Feel how

they bind together to hold you up and keep you connected,
then feel them relax. Next feel your blood: Is it pumping to the
same beat as the drum or going at its own rhythm? Follow its
beat, as you feel your skin. Notice how the air, your clothes,
your own hair feel against it. Now, push just beyond that
into the space just outside your body. Do you feel that power
surrounding you? Doesn't it feel incredible? This power is
always surrounding you, and you are just learning how to feel
it now.

- Stay in that place just outside your body and visualize yourself
  as you are laying or sitting. Start to see a little light come up
  from just below your feet and begin to move up your body.
- As this light travels up, see your body transforming into the
  animal you are going to use for soul flight. Your toes turn into
  talons, your skin into fur. Whatever it is, let yourself transform
  and let this transformation take as long as it needs to.
- Once you are fully transformed, let out a deep breath, and
  feel your soul and body disconnect. To me, the sensation
  is like the slight drop you get when an elevator starts
  descending.
- You may be seeing through your own eyes now, or you may
  be watching yourself from slightly above and behind
  like in a video game. Whatever happens is what is supposed
  to happen.

- From here, you can let yourself journey and travel wherever you decide to go. Sometimes soul flight can be directed toward a purpose, but I actually recommend flying just to fly the first few times to get used to it.
- When the bell rings or the timer goes off and it's time to return to your body, try not to rush. Visualize yourself again, and just like before let a light scan over you and transform you back into your human form, only this time start with your head and end with your feet.
- Write down everything you saw, even if it sounds silly now that you are back in "the real world." You may see symbols, patterns, or ideas pop up in your waking life that you first saw while flying. Pay attention to and follow these symbols.
- Afterward, I recommend you ground yourself back in this reality by drinking some water and having a snack.

You'll notice all I'm giving you here is a technique for flying, but not a guide of where to fly or what to do while you are there. That's because your reasons for journeying are going to be determined by what you or your community needs, and I don't want to limit you by just giving you one example. You can use this technique to supplement any of the other exercises in this book, and I recommend you do that once you get them down! Think of it this way—I just taught you how to operate a car, now it's up to you to drive it.

✳ ✳ ✳

CHAPTER 4

The Pathways
OF POWER

Whew! After the psychedelic chapter we just had, it's time to come crashing back to earth. It's all well and good to learn the secrets of the universe and fly to other dimensions, but if you don't bring that knowledge home and use it in this world, what's the point?

Back in chapter 1 (see page 2) I said magic is about recognizing the paths power takes in all beings and things and working with that power to change the world. In the last chapter, I gave you a way to dive into that current of power and experience it firsthand. Now, we're going to look at ways to practically map and direct that power in the material plane.

* * *

INTRODUCTION TO POWER MAPPING

When activists encounter a problem they want to fix, we'll often use a thing called "power mapping" to figure out the ways that problem is manifesting, who has the power to fix it, and what power we have to use to accomplish our goals.

As we look at this, it's important to remember that really, really evil shit in the world is often confusing on purpose. If there's one thing I want you to take away from this book, it's that there are reasons behind everything, even stuff that looks dumb on the outside. Laws, tax codes, social dynamics, and policies are often constructed and written in ways that make them purposefully hard for the average person to grasp and then get mad about. Power mapping helps break these obfuscating walls down and reveals the hidden pathways through which power is shaping and manifesting the world around you. Most importantly, the tools you'll learn give you a diagram to change them.

I should also say that you can use the technique of power mapping to figure out what kind of magic you need to do, especially if you like really complicated magic where, all jokes aside, you basically have to be a lawyer in order to talk to demons.

＊＊＊

THE THREE FACES
OF POWER

Power, like I said, is in everything and in many ways *is* everything. You can seriously spend a lifetime meditating on and studying exactly what power is. Just look at the thousands of years of theological texts the Catholics alone have churned out.

For our purposes, we are going to look at just a few ways power tends to manifest politically. They are called the three faces of power (shout-out to my girl Hekate) and they are:

1. **Immediate:** Who is actually doing the thing? Is there a person using their power for better or worse? Where is the bad thing happening, and what can you do right now to stop it?
2. **Law:** How is this power working legally? How is the law upholding this power or preventing this power from manifesting?
3. **Culture:** What's the popular consensus on this power? What do people generally think when you bring an issue up with them?

You are probably going to choose one face of power to work with as an activist to try to get something changed, but ideally, you'd want to use all three.

Let's look at an example of power to see how this all operates: the patriarchy. Okay, that's a big one, and it's a power that encompasses a lot. So let's break the faces of its power down:

1. Who is actually performing the actions of the patriarchy? Who are the flesh and blood humans holding it up or tearing it down? Where is the patriarchy immediately being felt?

2. How does the patriarchy manifest through the law? What laws has it created in order to protect itself and gain more power? What laws work against it?

3. What do people think about the patriarchy? Sexism? Transphobia? Homophobia? How do these things manifest in culture?

See that? We're still dealing with a big scary thing, but now we've broken it down into more manageable ideas and components, and by looking at how it functions, we can see that the patriarchy can, in fact, be overcome. Power works in part because we don't think about it and, more importantly, because we don't name its manifestations. Remember, in magic, naming something gives you control of it (see page 43). So let's map out power, name the power in our world, and take it back like Rage Against The Machine told us to.

✳ ✳ ✳

THE SPECTRUM
OF ALLIES

In activism and magic we talk a lot about allies: beings and people who actively want to help us succeed in our goals. We also talk about enemies: those who actively want to see us fail.

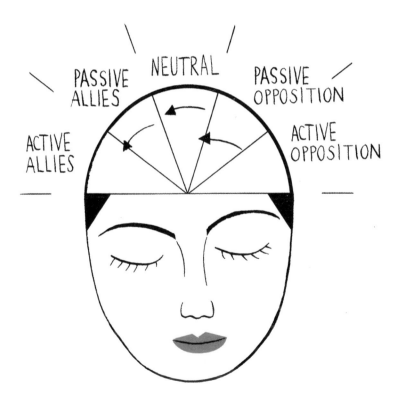

Most people and spirits though, fall somewhere on a spectrum. The spectrum of allies is something to keep in mind when you are out trying to win those in either realm over to your side. Ideally you will be trying to move people into being active allies, but the farther right they start out on the diagram, the more power it will take to bring someone over to your side, and the more interest they will have in seeing your defeat. I leave it up to you to decide who is worth your time and effort to move on this spectrum. I personally know people who were far-right organizers and avowed neo-Nazis whose hearts were turned away from hate, but I also know people who, for many reasons, I'm pretty sure will never be swayed from their current political beliefs. I am an activist because I believe people can change for the better, but in any situation you have to make that call as to who is worth trying to sway, why they are worthy of your energy, and how much power it will take to make them your ally.

✳ ✳ ✳

POWER MAPPING 101

Now that we've gone over the conceptual framework of power mapping, let's dig deeper into the steps you'll take to execute it yourself.

— Identify Goal —

1. **List long-term goals.** Go back to the dreaming chapter. This fight can't just be about one thing, or you'll end up fighting little battles all over the place and losing a lot of them. So think bigger! This is the fun part of power mapping. What is your absolute biggest, most ridiculous dream for the world? What does your utopia look like? Sit down and think about this, and let yourself dream big.

2. **List intermediate goals.** Okay, now that you have where you ideally want to end up, how do you get there? List out all the little goals that you think would lead to your big goal.

3. **What does victory look like?** In magic, you are going to get better results if you have a pretty clear picture of what you want. So what, exactly, do you want? What is victory going to look like in your little battle as opposed to the big fight? Dream about the feeling of victory, so you remember it when you get there.

— List Resources —

1. **What can you as an individual do or bring into action to advance the goal?** Can you protest? Donate money? Take time on the weekends to do work? We all have different skills and resources. List out yours!

2. **What can your organization do?** If you can, I really recommend getting involved in an organization if you plan on doing activist work. Unless you alone have some very incriminating video of a certain politician, there is honestly only so much one person can accomplish, and I don't want you to burn yourself out. You don't need to agree with the organization that you partner with 100 percent, but, as with magic, raising power is easier with many people working together. What resources does your group have?

— Identify Active & Passive Allies —

1. **Whose problem is this?** Go back to the spectrum of allies. You are trying to get people on your side. Who is affected by this problem? How do you make them see that this is their problem?

2. **What do they gain if they win?** You need to give people a reason to fight and a tangible thing that will be better when they win. What is it?

3. **What power do they have over the target?** We all have power as individuals, but our power and magic become stronger in groups What power do your allies have to make your target's life difficult until they give you what you want? Can they protest? Strike? Make calls? Engage in routine group rituals?

— Identify Active & Passive Enemies —

1. **What will your victory cost them?** If you win, what do your enemies lose? Money? Power? Influence? How much is winning this battle worth to them?
2. **What will they do to oppose you?** The bigger the stakes, the more your enemies will do to shut you down. This can be anything from just ignoring you and going around you to sending dogs and drones to attack you. Be prepared, but not paranoid.
3. **How strong are they?** List what resources your enemies have. Are we talking some bitter people on a community board or the governor here?
4. **How are they organized?** Organize yourself better than your enemy. Is this a small group of people or a large corporation? Are they based in one city or town, or are they global? Is their organization horizontally or vertically organized?

— Identify Targets —

A target is always a person, never an institution or system (unless we're talking about purely magical workings). When you do a spell, you will always be using a target, either yourself or someone else. To figure out an appropriate target, go back to the faces of power. Yes, you can protest racism, but how is the power of racism being made manifest in this world? Is a senator about to sign a racist law? Is a CEO about to build a corporate office that displaces low-income people of color? Is a TV show depicting a particular group in a demeaning way? Targets are the people with the power to stop one particular manifestation of something negative. Be careful when choosing your target that you consider the spectrum of allies. Some people you just can't win over. A real estate developer isn't going to not develop real estate—it's what they do—but a politician who doesn't know if they'll win reelection might be more open to hearing what you have to say (like how much you want them to stop that real estate developer through legislation). This is the idea behind electing someone on "your side" and then pressuring them into doing what you want. You elect them because, hopefully, you know they can be moved in a way that a politician on "the other side" couldn't be.

Primary Targets

1. **Who has the power to give you what you want?** Remember the spectrum of allies. You aren't going to change the essential nature of power that certain positions give people, so who can help you?
2. **What power do you have over them?** Is your target up for reelection? Are they looking to improve their public image? Are they likely to cave to sustained protests or actions?

Secondary Targets

1. **Who has the power over the people with the power to give you what you want?** Who are this person's supporters? Donors? Fans? Constituents? Customers? Can they be changed?
2. **What power do you have over them?** Are they aware there is a

problem with your target or that you want them to take action? Are they your coworkers or neighbors? What is the power relationship between you and the people who uphold your target?

— Tactics —

So you have your problem, goal, and target all mapped out—now you're going to do something about it! Tactics are how you go about actually demanding and creating change. Maybe you want to keep it purely magical through public ritual or group sigil work (more on that in a sec, or check out page 96), or maybe you want to be more traditional and stick to protests and letter writing. You and your allies are probably going to use what's called a "diversity of tactics." That means you may be working on getting someone elected, while your friend works on creating an urban farm. These strategies may seem totally different, but just like in magic, different spells can be used to create the same outcome. If you do your work while dreaming the same dream as others, you are both working toward the same goal.

There are some important things to keep in mind when choosing your tactics. Make sure they are:

- **In context.** Perhaps a Black Lives Matter protest isn't the place to show up with a "Save the Whales" sign. Keep in mind the thing you are fighting for and the conditions you are fighting under.
- **Flexible.** Remember that conditions change! If the place where you were going to protest gets shut down, what then? What if your candidate loses the election? If you can't get the projector to work or the banner to drop, is your whole action ruined? Always have a plan B.

- **Directed at specific targets.** "We want X to do/stop doing Y, and we won't stop causing a ruckus until it happens" is much clearer to onlookers than a sign that says "I'm mad." You may laugh, but I have seen this sign at real protests. Think of taking protest action like physics—if you scatter your power, you can't apply the pressure you need to move forward. If you throw all your power at one target, you have a much higher chance of pushing them where you want them to go.
- **Reasonable to those performing the tactics.** People doing the ritual, action, or protest should know why they are doing it, the meaning behind their actions, and what they hope to achieve with them. We live in an era where anyone can get on Facebook and make a protest, but we've also seen that those don't tend to work because the clarity of the dream and goal isn't there.
- **Backed up by a specific form of power.** One person screaming outside the White House isn't going to do much. If they are famous, maybe it does a bit more. If there are thousands of people, it might do even more, and if those thousands of people threaten to use their power, it might just work. Here are some examples of tactics that are backed by political embodiments of power:
  - Media events

- Public hearings
- Strikes
- Lawsuits
- Elections
- Protests
- Direct action
- Voting

That last one is super-important. If there's one thing from this chapter I want to yell in your face, tattoo on your chest, call you three times a day about, or stand outside your window with a boom box playing on repeat to help you remember, it's this: Voting is a tactic, not a strategy. Once more in case you're speed-reading: *Voting is a tactic, not a strategy*. Voting is lighting a candle, not doing candle magic. Voting is reciting words, not doing a spell. You must put the correct meaning on it and connect voting to a larger narrative to be effective. If you do decide to vote, always make sure it's *one* tactic you are using in a larger strategy of transformation, but there's a reason why movements or ideas that rely solely on voting usually fail—because the people who put that candidate in office confused tactics and strategies. Their enemies, I assure you, did not.

* * *

The Battle in Seattle

The 1999 World Trade Organization (WTO) protests, otherwise known as "The Seattle Protests" but also known by the much cooler name "The Battle in Seattle,"[*] were some of the most—and least—successful actions you've never heard of. Activists were able to achieve a great short-term goal—halting the WTO's final meeting of the millennium, while showcasing and elevating the fears and anger people all over the world had about the new organization and the spread of globalization. It also changed how large-scale mobilizations would be undertaken by activists and how they would be handled by the state. It's a great example of the power-mapping technique you just learned and why you need the kind of vision that magic can give you to make it all work.

But first, let's have some context!

The World Trade Organization was created in 1994, with the goal of managing trade globally. What does that mean? It means that the WTO can override the labor or environmental protections set up by a country if it thinks those laws interfere with another country's ability to buy and trade stuff with others. Under the rules of the WTO, countries can't block what companies can or can't come into their countries or how the

---

[*] This is also the name of a movie about this very protest. Unless Channing Tatum dressed as a cop being yelled at by a guy dressed as a sea turtle is a very specific kink you have, you can skip it.

factories those companies set up are always run. The WTO's system frees up the movement of money, but not people, which means you might live in a country that loses a lot of cash to another country because of globalization, but you can't necessarily move to follow that money. Not surprisingly, this sort of system often ends up benefiting countries with lots of money, which want to buy things cheaply and sell them for a profit, while paying people little to no money to make them, and hurts countries that want to protect their workers and, say, rain forests. The people making the decisions in the WTO aren't elected by people in the countries they represent.

I hope you understand that I don't really have enough space to line out all the complex nonsense of 1990s trade deals (remember, this book is being written by a witch who had to repeat math, twice), but given even that tiny bit of information, you can probably see why at the time people weren't big fans of this new kid on the block. Workers were afraid wages would drop or jobs would get taken away altogether; environmentalists feared further destruction of the planet; and civil rights groups worried this would further disempower women and people of color all over the world. Activists knew that the WTO was going to have its final meeting of the millennium in Seattle on November 30, 1999, and they decided this was the place to make themselves heard.

So activists came up with an *immediate goal* to shut down the WTO meetings. They spent months ahead of time *listing out their resources*, like how many people they could get there, what those people were willing to do, and what power each group had. *The spectrum of allies* shifted during the protests in incredible ways, when people and groups that at best didn't think they had anything in common, and at worst thought they were enemies, started fighting alongside each other. The best example of this was when one large group of activists was arrested and kept from seeing a lawyer, the Seattle unions shut down the ports until they were released. Likewise, who people thought were their *enemies* shifted as a result of the protest. When cops started using pepper spray not just on peaceful protestors, but on holiday shoppers and your average Joe, the protests grew larger as outrage increased in Seattle in general. The *tactics* people used were diverse and flexible, encompassing everything from protesting to getting arrested to shutting down whole streets and neighborhoods to concerts and dance parties.

The result of all this was, in the short term, success. Over five days protesters refused to back off despite pepper spray, tear gas, and baton beatings, and the WTO meeting was shut down. The world was suddenly aware that this organization existed at all, when almost no one had given it a second thought before.

On the other hand, everyone has moments where they look back and realize they should have done something differently. The Battle in Seattle was this kind of moment on a global scale—a potential turning point in the fight against the Disenchanted World that went slightly awry. The activists who shut down the WTO meeting had a great understanding of power in the short term and great foresight for the future, so what went wrong?

Let's go back and look at the weak spots in the spell these activists were trying to weave. Because remember, all protests are spells. If you look at the power map for the WTO protests, you'll see a couple of things missing.

One is that it's really hard to create a massive paradigm shift or challenge consensus reality (for a refresher, see page 36) if you can't name where the power that is holding up that reality emanates from. Remember how Isis was only able to draw the poison out of Ra once she learned his true name? You must name the power you are opposing and you and your allies must use the same name, or else your magic will fail.

The other hole that stands out in the Battle in Seattle's power map is the lack of a clear end goal. What did final victory look like to those protesting? I'm sure specific groups had ideas, but while there was cooperation on the ground, activists never seemed to unite their dreams.

The next exercise will cover this in a bit more depth, but for now just remember that in magic, it is important to have a clearly defined goal that you are working toward. The WTO protests themselves had this, but the movement didn't. People weren't dreaming the same dream.

There were a lot of things people *wanted* from the Seattle protests, and just one they didn't want. The list of yeses goes on and on, but the list of noes was short: no WTO. Specifically, the protesters didn't want that WTO meeting in Seattle to happen.

But what then? Where was the big "yes" to come about after? Some wanted to put pressure on elected officials to curtail the power of the WTO, while others wanted it gone altogether. Other groups wanted nothing to do with politicians and wanted to end not just the WTO, but capitalism and the state as well. Some of these ideas can go together, but I'm sure you can see how others simply can't.

The protesters successfully disrupted the WTO meeting they were united against, but could not follow up with a big-picture win because they hadn't come together on what that would look like. I think the name "The Battle in Seattle" is pretty apt here, since a battle implies one fight in a series of fights that make up a war that, ideally, you win. What should have been one siege in a bigger campaign became a war all on its own, so any long-term goals or dreams were bound to fail.

One of the best techniques I've found in magic is to always see your work as part of a bigger story. In politics, we might say that this is you being guided by an ideology, while in magic we might call this fitting your work into a paradigm. Whatever you decide to call it, making your mind think this way is going to keep you from feeling like you are fighting random battles and putting out fires all over the place and will instead make you believe that you are actually working toward something as inevitable as the final chapter of a book.

I get that this chapter may come across as less "magical" than the others, but that's only because we aren't used to looking at reality as something fundamentally magical. Reality is malleable, like the code in a computer. It's both highly structured and highly able to be fucked with. Once you start to see the pathways of power in your life and how easily they can be rerouted or transformed, you can start to use this to effect political change.

If you're still a little unsure of how to blend these lines of thought together, don't worry: It can take a little bit of time to rewire your brain. And one thing I've found that really helps in getting all this to click together is actually seeing it work. Our minds have this incredible power to shape reality, and we should use that power for good. That all sounds great, but unless you've actually felt magic having an impact in the world, it maybe sounds more like a cool idea and less like an awesome reality.

Sigils are one of my favorite ways to introduce someone to magic because they are easy to make, highly customizable, and so effective they can easily become a cornerstone of your practice. Seriously, you get so much bang for your buck with sigils it almost feels like cheating.

Some background before we get started: The idea of sigils can be traced far into history. The ancient Norse used to combine runes together to create spells and magical symbols, and in the nineteenth century an occultist and artist named Austin Osman Spare[*] coined the word *sigil* as a thoughtform, or a spell condensed into a symbol. Sigils are one of the main tools of chaos magic(k), which due to its individualistic and customizable attitude, I like to think of as the little brother of witchcraft.

Symbols have a ton of power. Think about a stoplight for a moment. It's a magical symbol! You see it turn red, and you stop (most of the time); you see it turn green, and you go. You've probably even done this when you've been alone and you knew there weren't any cops or traffic cameras around. It's not just force of habit that makes you behave like this—that symbol is actually compelling you on a subconscious level to act a certain way and think certain things. It has cultural and legal powers backing it up, but the actual thing that gives it power is belief, aka magic.

With sigils, you are making your own symbol that represents the reality you want to see around you. They are a way of hacking that part of your brain that makes reality, by getting into your subconscious and making your intentions just as real as the power of that stoplight. We're going to use sigils to help you with the power mapping we've already gone over, now in the service of achieving your activist goals.

For this, you will need:

---

[*] Cool story time: Spare was so popular with occultists during his time that a guy you may have heard of named Adolf Hitler asked him for a portrait. Spare, noted badass and "sexual deviant," refused, saying "If you are superman, let me be forever animal."

☾ A piece of paper

☾ A pen

Really, you can use any art supplies to make a sigil. Paint them on your nails before painting them over, draw them on the walls of your apartment before covering them up with pictures or paint, spray-paint them somewhere. There are even programs online that will generate them for you. (And we'll go over why you cover them up in just a moment.)

We're going to keep it simple for now, but feel free to mix it up however you want once you get it down.

Before you make your first sigil, think about what you want. Actually, scratch that, think about *how* you think about the things you want. Do your wants and desires feel like some far-off thing that you'll never attain? Do they feel like things other people get to have, but that you somehow don't deserve? The first step is to stop thinking this way, especially when making sigils. You are programming a thoughtform right now, making your own reality even as you read this book. You don't want your reality to be stuck in the *wanting* phase forever. Sigils are going to give you exactly what you ask for—so how you ask really matters.

In magic in general, it's the best practice to act like the reality you want has already come to pass when doing a spell. So, instead of saying "I want to be famous," you would say "I am famous." Dress your candles for the life you want, not the one you have.

Try this for a week: Pay attention, without judgment, to how you want things. When you're getting ready for your day, driving in your car, or walking down the street and have nothing but you and your thoughts, how do you think?

Do you say:

> This week is going to suck.

Instead of:

> This week will be hard,
> but I can face its challenges.

Or:

> I'm sick.

Instead of:

> I'm getting better, or I've got health
> problems, but I'm taking care of my body and
> addressing its needs.

Or:

> This city/country/world sucks.

Instead of:

> This place does suck, but my friends and I have
> the power to make it better and we will.

Notice, I'm not telling you to live in a fantasy and act like you don't have problems. I'm asking you to think more positively and actively about how those problems will be faced and overcome, as if those positive outcomes are just as inevitable as the current crappy situation. We are using magic to fix the wrongs of the world, not act like they don't exist.

Once you've gotten the hang of asking for what you want and thinking along better lines, look back at the power map you've created. At every step ask yourself and your friends: What do we want? What are we asking for? What challenges are we facing? Once you have those boiled down to your essential desire, it's time to make your sigil.

After you've dreamed big about the world you want to live in, decide on a step that you and your friends can take toward that world. For this, let's imagine you want to open a community farm and garden. It will be a place for people in your community to grow their own food, for kids to learn about plants and nature, and for people to hang out and meet up without having to pay.

Great! Let's break that down into a simple statement of intent:

We want a farm that will serve our community and uplift the people in it.

Now, take out the wanting:

We will build a farm that will serve our community and uplift the people in it.

You can even take out the "will" and place it in the present tense if you want:

This land is now a farm that will serve our community and uplift the people in it.

Here's the most common way to make a sigil from this:

• Take out your pen and paper and write your statement down.
• Take out all the repeating letters and the vowels.

So for this statement, you should have something that looks like this:

T H S L N D W F R M V C Y*P

• Now put those letters together in different combinations until you've come up with a symbol that you like. By the end it will probably look way more like a cool magic symbol than a bunch of letters smashed together. Here's an example of how I made a sigil out of the letters above:

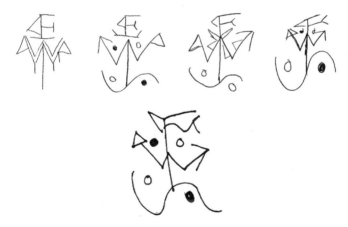

This is the method developed by occultist and comic book author Grant Morrison, but it's not the only way to get the

---

* Sometimes Y, depending on how it is used.

letters you need. If you want to use the first letter in every word or keep some vowels that really do it for you (I love the letter A and normally don't take it out when I do sigil work), you should do it! This is about hacking *your* brain and *your* reality, so feel free to personalize it.

Once you have your sigil, it's time to charge it! I'm using *charge* in its chaos magic and witchcraft meaning. By that I am saying you want to charge it, like a battery, to give it power and a life of its own, but you also want to give it a charge, or a direction of what to do. In this case, your direction will probably be something like "I charge you to make *X* a reality."

You can charge a sigil using anything. Literally—anything. I've charged sigils through Instagram, house parties, and candles. I've heard of people doing it through music, theater, and interpretive dance. What you're trying to do is raise and release power while keeping your desired outcome in mind. Remember, sigils are a creative form of magic. If you want to charge your sigil by making it part of your music, dance, or artistic craft, by all means go for it.

Then once you have your sigil made, you want to forget about it—or at least forget about its meaning. Remember the stoplight? Part of the power of that symbol is that you notice it without noticing it; it's so normal and bland that you don't think about the huge power it has over you.

So once you've charged your sigil, take it and put it somewhere where you'll see it often—or at least know it's there—but the exact meaning can be forgotten over time. That's where covering it up comes in. Or you can also place it someplace where you will only notice it peripherally. Put it on your mirror, hang it by your door, throw it under the rug, bury it in the garden, or paint it on a protest sign. You want to absorb it into your very being so that the magic starts to work without you "doing" anything.

* * *

CHAPTER 5

Witches and
WILDERNESS

Remember chapter 1? We were all so young and innocent back then, weren't we? Remember how I also said that one of the first things the modern ruling class had to take control of was the land and, by extension, witches? Well it's about time we talk about liberating that land, don't you think?

Witches get their power from a connection with the land, but what the heck does that actually mean? In the Disenchanted World we're all disconnected from our bodies, each other, and especially the land. In this chapter we're going to talk about what that actually looks like and how to fix it.

How do you kill gods? You put a price tag on them. And that is what has happened to wilderness all over the world. This attack is still going on, even in places that don't seem very "wild" to most.

I'm not just talking about mountains and rivers and forests here, although those are definitely under attack. I'm talking about the idea of "wildness" itself. Witches started to burn when the land became something to be sold and bought. Today this seizing of the commons isn't just happening to the land, but anything in our society without a price tag or ability to fit nicely into a premade box. The Disenchanted World simply can't deal with people, places, or ideas being wild. Politically, this is and will probably always be the central dividing line: Left vs. right is freedom vs. authority, liberty vs. hierarchy, wilderness vs. confinement. I think we know where witches should stand.

Whatever your practice ends up looking like, I'd like to return to your magic the idea of wilderness. No, this doesn't mean you have to pretend you were born on a mountainside during a thunderstorm and that your mom is actually a wolf and you can talk to animals like the girl from the *Wild Thornberrys*. It means being okay with not all questions, especially spiritual ones, being answered. It means allowing some things to be nameless, uncharted, free. It means recognizing that surrendering your control to nature does not surrender your power and in fact allows you to see that the divide between nature and you was a fake one all along!

Let's talk about ways to connect deeper to the land, nature, and its spirits and about what an earth-based revolution can look like.

* * *

ALLIES ARE EVERYWHERE

You may remember that earlier in this book I spoke about animism. I myself am an animist, but what is that actually, and how does it fit into activism?

The Disenchanted World is a desecrated one, meaning literally everything has been made unsacred—all the magic and spirits have been sucked out of it.

Not everyone can get along in a world that wants to chew up everything and make it into profit, so the people who run the world act like that sacredness doesn't exist. Thinking that plants, animals, and even people are more than the sum of their atoms and whatnots and are therefore worth fighting for beyond their just being anonymous "resources" is viewed as stupid or childish by many, but we witches know better. It's not enough just to save a forest because of some complex calculation about how much carbon it eats or how much oxygen it produces. It's worth protecting because that forest has a spirit and rights like any of us, rights that aren't tied to its ability to "work" for us. Rights should *never* be tied to work or how usefully you can be exploited by someone else.

Animism isn't really a religion, and it's not really a set practice either. Like witchcraft, it can be a little hard to explain what you mean when you identify that way without going through a whole lesson in anthropology and history. I'll try to keep it short and say that animism, much like witchcraft, is a philosophy that's less about what you think about the world and more about how you interact with it. It's about what you do, and animism is simply saying that the world is a living thing that we can have a conversation and healthy relationship with. How you go about doing that is going to be up to you.

How this relates to magic is pretty straightforward. But how this relates to our understanding of politics is a little more complicated and for sure going to be interpreted in a bunch of different ways. My own hot take is that this inherent spirituality and interconnectedness form the missing piece of a lot of environmental movements. We are fighting against the desecration of the natural world and the destruction of all life within it, but how can we do that when both sides just look at nature as a bunch of . . . stuff? How are we different, then, at the end of the day?

To dive into this, I'm going to need to touch on a topic I've avoided so far. I've resisted talking about it because, well, the whole thing annoys me, and also because I think it's a cover for the real power in the Disenchanted World—capital—but as is so often the case with our opposition, this subject has things to teach us. I'm speaking about the religious right, specifically as it operates in the USofA. As a movement, the religious right has been incredibly successful. Look at all those Supreme Court justices! Take a gander at those anti-LGBTQ laws! Just sit back in awe of the sweeping victories of the "right" "to" "life" movement! I don't like them, but damn do those fuckers get shit done.

Why are they so successful when poll after poll show Americans becoming less religious—especially traditionally so—more tolerant of queerness, and more okay with the crazy idea that women are humans? Well, magic, is one reason. They have the power of unshaken belief that they are fighting for something bigger on their side. So, to circle back, what do environmentalists fight for? Who do we fight for?

I can't separate my animism from my understanding of politics or my activism. When we look at the struggle of power in the world and how we are so close to ecological collapse, I can't help but hear all those old warnings about what would happen if the disrespected spirits of a place came back to haunt us. Or, when I think about the forest I grew up in and cry because I know climate change will likely destroy it, I don't just cry because the land is beautiful or I have happy memories there. I cry because I know my friends are dying.

And that right there is why I think having a living, animistic relationship with the world is so vital to your witchy activism. Break it down to its absolute most material, utilitarian function for a second: You are going to fight longer, harder, and with a greater chance of success if you are fighting for your friends, not just a pile of pretty rocks.

* * *

LISTEN TO THE LAND

We make a big to-do in the witchy/pagan/new age/whatever-the-kids-are-calling-it-these-days scene about being "earth-based," but what that means seems up for debate.

To some it means looking at the earth as a mother goddess that women are uniquely connected to. Something about this conception has always rubbed me the wrong way. Just like I roll my eyes when people say there's only one god and he's some bearded dude sitting on a cloud, why does nature have to be a white woman with long hair and conveniently placed leaves? If we're talking all of existence, doesn't gendering that just narrow it down? Plus what about the women who don't want babies or don't have built-in baby incubators?

So maybe the earth, or nature, is not a goddess lady (to be clear, I don't know). Maybe it's power, a *force* like we've been talking about. That feels a bit better, right? Picky me, I'm still rubbed the wrong way by this sometimes. It makes people think that nature is all peaceful and calm, when these days I don't know how true that is.

Just to be clear, I really am a fan of walking around the woods and meditating. It's where I feel the most peaceful and connected. I fully plan on disappearing from the world to live in a cabin someday, so I can spend all my time doing this. I'm just waiting till I'm appropriately wizened. I think nature strives for balance, and, yes, a current of peace can run through that. But right now that balance has been so thoroughly messed up by us humans, there are very few places left where the land feels at peace.

In the appendix to this book (see page 136), you can find an exercise to connect with the land you live on and learn to talk to it better. When we do this, I think it's very important that we really listen, not just hear what we want to or think we are "supposed" to hear. The earth is under attack, and when something is under attack, it isn't usually in such a great mood. Wherever you are—in a city, a town, a tent in the wilderness—I hope you use your gifts as a witch and really listen to what the land is telling you. And if it tells you it is sick, I hope you'll keep using your powers to help it.

Land spirits, in my experience, form the backdrop to all the other bits of magic people do, whether you know it or not. This relationship—like any others you have—will only grow stronger if you pay attention to it and keep the conversation going. Witchcraft connects us to the circle of life (cue the music), and it's not just okay to say that life isn't so great where you are—it's necessary! Most people can't understand what the land is trying to tell them. You'd think that hurricanes, wildfires, tsunamis, and mass extinction would be enough of a wake-up call, but some folks just don't listen.

If you can hear the voice of the land, it's your job as a witch to speak for it to those who can't. I might be a total hippie, but I really do think that love is the goal of life and peace and love are goals we need to all be striving for. (I'm a sap, get over it.)

The problem with peace, especially when it comes to the land, is people think of it is as a means and not an end. It can be both, but you may need to cause some disruption, ruffle some feathers, and topple some kings so that the scales can be balanced and peace can return. I'm not going to tell you exactly how to do that here—I've already given you some homework in this book and I believe in using a diversity of tactics. What I will say is that it's a tragedy that we don't get the natural world so many of our magical traditions were born out of—and we never will. There are spirits you will never talk to and animals that go extinct every day. Children are born with poison in their blood, lead in their water, and chemicals filling their lungs with their first breath of air. This is not peace; this is a war on all of us.

Discomfort is not good, but it is good to sit with and consider it. At this point in the book, I think you've learned a lot. You've learned that things don't have to be the way they are, that another world is possible, that we have the power to create that world, and that as witches we must speak the words the dying earth cannot. Listen, feel, speak.

* * *

The Zapatistas

We are so separated from our land it can sometimes be really hard to know how to fight for it. It can be even harder to know how to do this the right way. Some people think that loving where you are from means hating everywhere else or that no one from those "other" places should come over to "your" turf. The globalization we talked about with the Battle in Seattle (see page 90) can be really scary to people, because it means you may lose your culture, language, and way of life. But hunkering down and telling all those "others" to get out misses the beautiful connection that nature and the knowledge of power give us.

Yes, you may be more connected to the place where you live than a place halfway around the globe, but we all share and cocreate this world together. On top of that, our oppressors are often the same people, not each other. Was it an immigrant's fault for taking your job? Or was it your boss's fault for screwing both of you over by firing you and paying that immigrant less money to work more? And why is that person you are demonizing here to begin with? Do they have a family thousands of miles away they would rather be with, but can't because of a war in their country that was started by a bunch of even *bigger* bosses?

A group that really understands this balance, and whose fight is deeply inspirational, is the Zapatistas of Mexico. The

Zapatistas are a revolutionary organization in the southern
state of Chiapas, who in 1994 held an uprising and took back
control of much of their traditional Mayan territory from
the Mexican government. To this day they hold most of this
territory and have built schools and medical centers in each
of their towns. Women make up half the leadership roles, and
I highly recommend you check out the EZLN Revolutionary
Women's Law that all Zapatistas follow.

So how did the Zapatistas achieve this? They were rebelling against trade deals like NAFTA and organizations like the WTO, which threatened their way of life and their ability to control their own destiny. For instance, the corn they grow, which not only forms a staple of their diet and economy, but is filled with spiritual significance, was at risk of being overwhelmed by cheap corn imported from the United States. This would have meant that not only would many people, indigenous and otherwise, be plunged into poverty, but because of this poverty they would have been further subject to the whims of a government which they viewed as bad and corrupt. Their rebellion wasn't just against a policy or politician, but against a world that made such things possible. Like at Standing Rock, they flipped the way things were normally done on its head. Their attitude is in many ways encapsulated by one sign on a road leading into a Zapatista village, which reads "You are in Zapatista rebel territory. Here the people give the orders and the government obeys."

The Zapatistas are guided by their indigenous knowledge and spirituality, and instead of going around the world starting revolutions, they hope others will simply be inspired by the lives they have chosen to lead and dream new lives into reality in their own countries aligning with their own values.

In their first year of independence, the Zapatistas invited people from around the world to come to Chiapas, learn about what they were doing there, and take that knowledge back home. Here is an excerpt of a transcript that was written after that first meeting, called "The 2nd Declaration of La Realidad":

As to what happened in these days, much will be written later. Today we can say that we are certain of at least one thing. A dream dreamed in the five continents can come to make itself real in R/reality. Who now will be able to tell us that dreaming is lovely but futile? Who now will be able to argue that dreams, however many the dreamers, cannot become a reality?

How is joy dreamed in Africa? What marvels walk in the European dream? How many tomorrows does the dream enclose in Asia? To what music does the American dream dance? How does the heart speak that dreams in Oceania? To whom does it matter how and what we dream here or in any part of the world? Who are they who dare to convene with their dream all the dreams of the world? What's happening in the mountains of the Mexican Southeast that finds echo and mirror in the streets of Europe, suburbs of Asia, rural areas of America, townships of Africa, and houses of Oceania? What's happening with the peoples of these five continents that, so we are all told, only encountered each other to make war or compete? Wasn't this turn of the century synonymous with despair, bitterness, and cynicism? From where and how did all these dreams arrive at reality? . . .

> May the five continents speak and everyone listen. May humanity suspend for a moment its silence of shame and anguish. May humanity speak. May humanity listen. . . . In the world of those who live in the Power and kill for the Power, the human being doesn't fit, there is no space for hope, no place for tomorrow. Slavery or death is the alternative that their world offers all worlds. . . .
>
> But there are those who do not resign themselves, there are those who decide to be uncomfortable, there are those who do not sell themselves, there are those who do not surrender themselves. There are, around the world, those who resist being annihilated in this war. There are those who decide to fight.
>
> In any place in the world, anytime, any man or woman rebels to the point of tearing off the clothes that resignation has woven for them and that cynicism has dyed grey. Any man, any woman, of whatever colour in whatever tongue, says and says to himself, to herself, "Enough already"—Ya Basta!

You better believe it took all my strength to not just copy/paste the whole dang thing into this book. Thankfully though, the internet is a thing that exists, and I really urge you to read the rest there.

The Zapatistas show us a way to love and care for your land and fight to defend it, without it being an exclusive club only people who look like you belong to. The Zapatistas, from the very beginning, saw their movement as international and multiracial. They reached out to people from all over the world to come and learn from them and vice versa, with the dream of liberating all people wherever they are. This is part of something called "internationalism" which means working together on common goals across borders. It's a beautiful way of looking at the world and finding common ground with other people in it. You're basically saying "I'm not you, but I see my struggle in your struggle, and I'm going to help you with it." The Zapatistas see their fight embodied all over the world.

I wanted to include the Zapatistas as my last example of magical activism because I think they embody the lessons from each section of this book. How are you initiating other people and yourself into your movement? How is your struggle connected to the land? How are you living your magic? And how are your dreams connected to the dreams of others?

MAGIC IN ACTION
PROTEST AS RITUAL

Are you inspired yet? Has this book got you all fired up to go out and transform the world! Alright! Let's do one last exercise to bring it all home.

Like we talked about in chapter 4, there's almost no limit to the list of tactics you can use when trying to make your political dreams a reality, just like there's no limit to how many spells you could do.

We're going to talk about protesting because it's popular and as a tactic requires a bit more finesse than going to a voting booth and checking off a box. I'm using the term *protest* very loosely. So if you want to apply this lesson to direct action, occupations, letter-writing campaigns, or anything else you can dream up, go for it!

Now, let's get one thing straight: The idea that humans are all rational actors guided by pure reason is, to put it nicely, bullshit. We are creatures of myth and story, compelled to action through narrative. If this gets you down, it really shouldn't! This is where the power of ritual comes from.

Ritual is the act of embodying a story. It is weaving a spell, with your body, mind, and words acting as one. When you protest, demonstrate, do direct action, or march, you are telling a story and asking people to become a character in it. You are enacting a ritual.

Protest and direct action are public rituals. This is what I usually tell people who say you have to do your magic in secret only. Look, there's a lot about my magical practice that I just can't tell you and have to keep secret in order to maintain its power, but to say all magic, or all magical rituals, must be done in absolute secrecy to be effective is, I think, a shortsighted view of this thing that literally makes up all of reality.

We engage in public magic rituals all the time in politics. From the inauguration of world leaders to standing and singing national anthems to Election Day, we all live in a world whose very functioning is made by beliefs, and those beliefs are made real through public ritual. That's just the way the metaphysical cookie crumbles!

Once we understand this, we can choose how we want to create our own rituals of resistance, revolution, and transformation. After all, why should those in power get to have all the fun?

Turn back to the power-mapping section (see page 78). Let's say you and your friends have identified a common goal, a thing standing in the way of that goal, and a target you think can be moved to use their power to help you achieve your goal. After you've gone through and done all this, let's say you and your friends decide a protest or a direct action is the tactic you want to use to move this target. In that chapter, I gave you lots of practical advice for staying on message and ways to make your point clear. Now, I'm going to give you techniques for adding some magical oomph to the process.

Some stuff to consider when crafting your action:

☾ What is the story we are telling?

☾ Does our messaging convey this story well?

☾ Who is this for?

☾ Who is this against?

☾ What do we want the outcome of this to be?

And some stuff to consider when you are joining in:

☾ Before your action:

- Gather as many participants together as you can. Sit or stand in a circle and talk about your intentions for this action. Why are you here? Who are you fighting for? Speak their names aloud. If you cannot do this with others beforehand, do this by yourself.

- What do you personally plan on doing? What story are you helping to tell? What world do you hope to create?

- Are there physical talismans of the thing you are fighting for that you can wear during your action? This could be buttons and shirts with a message on it, but if those aren't available to you, get creative! Put dirt from the land you are fighting for in your shoe, or write a loved one's name on your arm. Bring the spirit of what you are fighting for with you.

- If you are doing an action that involves your body directly, go back to the soul flight exercise in chapter 3 (see page 70), and just do the first part. Your body is a gift you are about to use in service of something

beautiful. Take time to thank and honor your body,
your voice, your mind.

- If you are with other people, hold hands and form
  a circle. Do the Meditation 101 exercise from the
  appendix (see page 129) together. Chant words of
  power and feel the power of your group. You are here
  for each other, as well as with each other. For the next
  few hours, this is your family.

☾ During your action:

- There is a good chance you may be mocked or that
  people may try to get you to leave. If you don't want
  to leave and you know the legal consequences of not
  leaving, take a deep breath. Imagine yourself as a tree
  firmly rooted in place, feel roots growing beneath your
  feet. This will ground you more firmly and make you
  harder to move.

- Don't get distracted. Give in to trolls or break up too
  soon, and you can disturb the flow of power that you
  are building.

- But having said that . . . be willing to let the spirit take
  its course. This doesn't mean that you should just do
  whatever with no plan. It does mean that protests,
  especially big ones, can take on a life of their own—
  literally and magically—and you have to be flexible.
  If it looks like people are going to storm the Winter
  Palace and there's no stopping them, you have to make
  the call to either get out or keep people safe and the
  message on point while this happens.

- If you can't physically be there, how can you help? Can you follow on social media from home and keep your friends up to date on developments? Can you do protective spells from a distance?

☾ After your action:
- It's always good to engage in aftercare after any activity that engages body and spirit. You need to come back down to earth, even if you only left for a bit. Protest, meditation, magic, sex—all of these engage us on multiple levels of being and power, and we have to take care of ourselves in different ways as we recalibrate.
- Take time to attend to your body. You probably need water, food, and maybe a hug. Everyone's aftercare is going to look a little different, but besides the obvious things like drinking some water, having a snack, and fixing bruises or wounds you may have gotten, here's something to do: Take a deep breath and, without judgment, take stock of what you are feeling. Happy? Scared? Excited? Anxious? Whatever emotions you have, find where you are feeling them in your body and how they feel. For instance, I feel anxiety like a hamster running on a wheel in my chest, but for my friend it is like her hair is on fire. When you locate the emotion in your body, help your body move through it by giving it what it needs on a basic material level. Maybe a massage will help or just a good laugh. What you are trying to do is locate where negative feelings are clinging to you and help them move on.

- Once you feel more or less back to normal, talk to other people who engaged in protest with you about how they felt while it was going on and how they feel now. Was it scary? Exciting? Inspiring? Do you feel like you made a difference? Why and how?
- What next? How do you plan on continuing to build and grow the power you gathered today?
- Thank your ancestors and the spirits of the place you did your action on.

* * *

A Spellbook for
THE APOCALYPSE

Ooooh what a big scary name, right?

Don't worry, or maybe worry, but don't despair. People use the word *apocalypse* to mean the end of the world, but the term actually means "an uncovering" in Ancient Greek. In other words, just like the Tower card in tarot means destruction as well as revelation, the apocalypse is the end of the old world *and* the initiation into a new one. With that, let me be the first to welcome you to the apocalypse! Happy you could make it!

It might be obvious for me to say after you've read this whole book, but I don't think the way we've been doing witchy stuff over the last couple years is really sustainable anymore. That's why this book is filled with big words like *revolution* and *apocalypse*, because our witchcraft needs more of that stuff right now!

In that spirit, I wanted to include an offering of spells and rituals at the apocalypse of this book. You'll notice that lots of these rituals, like ones I've given you throughout this book, are similar to stuff that can be found elsewhere. Spoiler: I'm not the first person to put sigils or the Wheel of the Year in a book on witchcraft. The difference is in how we can start to think about these rituals and exercises, and what context we should put them in (i.e., the framework of the end of the freaking world).

So here is a little bit of magic to get you started on your revolutionary witchcraft journey! You'll notice that the rituals don't cost you a thing and I leave them open for you to put your own spirit and flare into. This is a spellbook, not a cookbook. Take it as inspiration, and then go wild.

* * *

MEDITATION 101

Wait! Come back! Don't skip this part!

Practically every beginner's book on magic contains a basic meditation technique. It's a proud tradition I intend to keep! That's because while there's a lot in magic you don't have to do, or can do your own way, knowing how to meditate is really the one thing you can't skip over. If you were to enter a painting competition, you could paint whatever you want, however you want, but you should know how to hold a brush first.

So why is meditation so fundamental to doing magic? Simply put, it's the basic tech you'll use for most of your magical work—your spiritual software, if you will. Meditation helps all of us focus our intentions, clear our minds, and get into a state of consciousness where we can receive and send messages to spirits, gods, and ancestors more easily. A daily meditative practice literally changes how your mind works, which as we've already discussed is a big part of magic. You don't have to reach a meditative state the "boring" way—i.e. sitting down and breathing— but this is the easiest method for most people. Once you get the hang of basic meditating, you'll start to see how other things you do like singing, dancing, drawing, or driving can also put you into a meditative state. After finding that out about yourself, you may learn your magic works better with one of these meditative states. If so, go for it and stay with it! For now though, we're going to stick to getting a general handle on things.

Here is a simple meditative technique. You can use this just to meditate but also to get you into the magical mind-set you'll need for the other exercises. We'll be using a breathing technique called the Fourfold Breath for this, but it's good to note that there are dozens of other breathing exercises to read up on too.

For ten minutes a day, every day if you can, sit down and do the following:

- Close your eyes and begin to clear your mind. Let thoughts fall away and bring your attention to your breath.
- If thoughts do come in, or you find your attention drifting, no worries! Just acknowledge the thought, let it go, and get back to your breathing.
- Breathe in through your nose for four seconds.
- Hold your breath for four seconds.
- Breathe out through your mouth for four seconds.
- Hold your breath for four seconds.
- Repeat.

And . . . that's it! See? It's so simple you might think it's fine to skip, or that I'm making too big a deal of it. Seriously, I'm not. It may be proof that the universe has a sense of humor, but the most mind-altering, magical thing you can do right now is also the simplest, available to you all the time, with no cost at all. Just sit and breathe.

* * *

THE TRANS RITE OF ANCESTOR ELEVATION

This ritual isn't mine, but I love it so much I wanted to include it here for all of you to try out! This ritual was concocted by the folks over at trans-rite.tumblr.com, and they were gracious enough to let me put it in this book. If this ritual excites you, please go check out their blog for more tips, prayers, and answered questions. Thanks y'all, you rock!

The Trans Rite of Ancestor Elevation is a nine-day ritual that takes place November 12–20. It was created by trans and gender nonconforming people to honor their ancestors of spirit who were lost to murder or suicide in the previous year, a sadly all too common occurrence these days. Hopefully you are reading this book during better times, but according to the ACLU as of my writing, one in four trans people, and most often trans women of color, report violence against them based on their gender, and much of this violence results in death or later suicide. In the face of so much horror and sadness, honoring the dead is not just a good practice; it might even be a necessary one. Rituals such as this provide healing to the dead. It helps the dead find peace instead of becoming angry, restless spirits. Consider that violence against trans people usually persists after death, through official reports often misgendering and using the "dead name" of a trans person. How can the dead ever rest if we cannot even call them by their proper name?

Remember back in chapter 1 where we talked about an ancestor practice not just being a way for you to pick up some cool undead relatives, but as a way to aid in healing the world from the trauma of the past and present? Yup, this right here is a great example of how that can look in practice. Cisgender people who wish to honor trans loved ones who have been killed, or aid in the elevation of trans ancestors, can participate as well.

For it you will need:

- ☾ A place to set up an altar
- ☾ A candle (preferably white)
- ☾ A cup for water
- ☾ A white cloth of some sort (bandanas or pride flags also work)
- ☾ Prayers, quotes, songs, or poems of your choosing
- ☾ Nine books with meaning to yourself or those you will be honoring
- ☾ Any offerings or symbols you wish to place on your altar. Some people put out hormone pill bottles/syringes, lipstick, prosthetics, patches, crystals, magical tools, etc. Flowers also always work in a pinch.

For this ritual, the altar you make will be set up on the floor. Lay down the white cloth on the floor to make your altar space for the next nine days. If you have to move it for some reason, that's okay, but try to do the ritual at the same time and place each day, without disturbing the altar if possible.

This ritual can be done alone or with a group of people. You can keep your altar simple or dress it up with flowers and pictures of the dead if you like. Go with what feels right to you. However, make sure you never place photos of living people on an altar to the dead, and do not eat or drink offerings left for them.

Alright, have you got your stuff ready? Here we go!

• For nine nights in a row, stand or sit before your altar. Give yourself a minute to breathe, meditate, and get into that good magic headspace using our Meditation 101 technique.

- Cleanse yourself in a way of your choosing. I personally like to burn mugwort, but cedar and rosemary along with many other plants also work great.
- Light the candle and offer a cup of water on the cloth. Don't start getting fancy on me here and leave out glasses of wine or other alcohol; water is what you want for this.
- Read the prayers, poems, or other writing you've prepared. You can switch up which prayers or readings you do nightly, but each night, start by saying the following prayer:

I call upon the ancestors of my line, the progenitors of my queer spirit, those who came before and laid the path behind them, the mighty transgender dead.

I call to your restlessness and your strife, the thread of pain that twists through your lives and your deaths, the thread that binds me to you.

I call upon the helping spirits who have stepped up to tend the line of the honored transgender dead, those who led in life and lead in death, those who offer the gift of their guidance and protection to the members of their family who have yet to find peace, to the troubled dead thirsting for care and to the weary living still battling each day.

(NAME), I call to you. Hail and welcome. I offer you honor and remembrance. I offer you love and devotion. I offer you praise and proclamation among the living to bring your legacy to your descendants.

I offer you cool water for your journey. **(Name any ancestral helping spirit, deity, or representatives you are personally honoring or working with in your ritual. The authors of this ritual have been invoking Marsha P. Johnson, Sylvia Ray Rivera, and Comrade Leslie Feinberg, and encourage people to do divination to confirm with any individual members of the line that they want to invoke that they are up for it.)**

I seek your guidance in elevating our troubled family. I seek the strength of your fury in my journey. I seek your hands on my shoulder as I hold our family's pain in my body and in my heart.

To the troubled transgender dead, I call to you. Hail and welcome. I offer you honor and remembrance. I offer you love and devotion. I offer you praise and proclamation among the living to bring your legacy to your descendants.

I offer you my will to fight in this world. I offer you my fists and my tools to build a world that would have been kind to you. I offer you a light to guide you to peace and music to dance you out of this cruel place. I offer you cool water for your journey. May you never thirst.

For other prayers and ideas, visit the official website for the Transgender Rite of Ancestor Elevation.

• After you've made your offerings and said your prayers, take one of the nine books you've chosen and stack it under the candle

and cup. By the end of nine nights, you should have nine books
stacked under this candle on your altar. See how this is literally
"elevating" the ancestors? This bit of the ritual is derived
from Afro-Caribbean spiritual traditions such as Santeria and
Espiritismo Cruzado. It serves to physically raise up the ancestors
alongside spiritually lifting them through prayer and ceremony.

- Before ending the ritual, take a moment to sit with the spirits,
  make offerings of song or speech, and thank them before blowing
  out the candle.
- Cleanse yourself at the end of each night of ritual.
- When it comes time to fill another cup of water, throw the water
  from the previous night on some plants or outside; don't dispose
  of it in the toilet.
- This ritual ends on the Trans Day of Remembrance, when the
  names of trans people who have died in the past year are read
  aloud. Do this at the end of your nine-day ritual as well.

TALKING TO
LAND SPIRITS

At the end of the day, we aren't something outside of nature fighting for nature. We are nature fighting for itself. Did I just blow your mind?

Connecting to the land we live on seems like a nice, but difficult idea to many. Yes, you could always just go to the park and run after squirrels, begging them to talk to you, but there are other people around and they're starting to get worried.

I kid, but talking to the land isn't always the same as talking to people. Imagine your ship sinks and you wash up on a deserted island with just one other person, and neither of you speaks the same language. You may learn bits and pieces of each other's words, but after awhile, you're going to have to find other ways to communicate. In my experience, this is a bit like talking to spirits of place.

To start making your own land language, you have to get comfortable with your intuition. Feel how your feelings make you feel—you feel me? This bit isn't so much a ritual, but more a foundation that you can build rituals off of. For this, pick a place you want to connect with. I recommend something near you, even just your neighborhood or backyard! Start with one place, and see what changes, or doesn't, when you apply this method to others.

- Get yourself a land journal and write in it as much as possible. Take quick notes on what feelings or vibes you get when you go to certain places. If you live in a city or big town, you can do this with neighborhoods, parks, and buildings.

- Go to a place you want to connect with and do the Meditation 101 exercise on page 129, even for five minutes.
- After your mind has been cleared out a bit, open it back up to freely associate. What things come to mind when you stand next to a certain tree? When you meditate next to a river? When you walk down a particular street? You'll start to find that some places are quiet for you while others are practically shouting. Don't force the quiet ones, especially when you are just getting started.
- Write down all the things that consistently spring to mind when you think of this place or visit it. Colors, symbols, music, movies—anything is fair game. Spirits, especially spirits of place, are going to try to talk to you in a language you can understand, and this is often going to be pictures in our head. Remember, it doesn't have to be "serious" or ancient things that come to you. Is there a song, even a pop song, which comes to mind every time you're happy and suddenly starts playing in your head when you visit a forest? Listen to that. Does it change by season? Time of day? Write it all down to start creating a personal land language you can use to speak with spirits of place.
- After you've made some personal assumptions and discoveries, research your place. Does anything from your visions or waking meditations line up with its history? Who were the original people who lived on that place? Do they still live there? Why or why not? What plants grow there? What animals live there? What folktales, legends, or myths have been told about this place?
- Now you can start talking. Wear those colors, sing those songs, put on that perfume, do whatever it is you feel "fits" when you go to that place. Eat food that's grown locally, if you can. Leave a penny,

or some kind of offering, for that place when you've had a very good day there. Blur the lines and deepen the connection between you and the land.

- Once you've got a language established, and know about the history of the land you're on, ask what the land wants from you. Sometimes this can be as simple as a thank-you and some offerings every now and then, sometimes you're going to find this place and its inhabitants face much bigger problems that you may want to help with. When you get here, go back to the power map to try to figure out what is wrong and how to help.

HACKING YOUR LOCAL SPELLBOOK

Have you ever noticed that recipes you get for spells are almost all exactly the same?

There are roses for love, sage for cleansing, and lavender for pretty much anything? I'm not saying these plants don't have power, but the mono-cropping of spellbooks is something I've gotten a little sick of.

There's something a little paint-by-numbers and, honestly, colonial feeling to it all. I've never even seen white sage grow in the wild, so why am I using it for cleansing if I know nothing about it or have no connection to it?

If we are going to do deep, transformative magic, we have to let our magic be transformed, and transform it ourselves.

So while you don't have to do this for every magical formula or spell you find in books out there, use this little method to personalize and reimagine your magic.

- Go online or pick up a guidebook on local plants and animals in your area. They are legion and often written by adorable men in sweaters or women in long floral dresses.
- Look up the lore of plants near you, and make a reference guide for yourself. For instance: mugwort = spirit contact, rosemary = cleansing. You get the idea. Write down any myths associated with the plant. What's its story?
- When a spell calls for plants or herbs to be used, pop open that guidebook. Does that plant grow near you? If so, can you harvest it yourself instead of going to the store?
- If it doesn't grow near you, check the personal guidebook you've

made. Is there a plant that does grow near you that does a similar thing? You can't always just copy/paste and replace every herb, but localizing the plants you use will help you connect to the spirit of place and help the earth out a bit. Why get herbs shipped to you from halfway around the world when you can go pick them in your backyard?

* * *

LAND ACKNOWLEDGMENT

This is an idea a number of indigenous activist groups have asked nonindigenous groups to incorporate into their meetings. I think it's great not just for meetings with you and your friends, but for performing before rituals too, so I'm giving it a shout-out here! A land acknowledgment is a statement made before a meeting, ceremony, or ritual that honors the indigenous people who once called—and likely still do—that land home before the settlers came. It also honors the land itself and thanks it for just being the MVP every day. It's a first, powerful step for healing the scars of the past and moving toward reconciliation.

Look up the history of the place you are organizing and activisting on. Did other people live there once? Were they kicked out in maybe not the nicest of ways? What was their name? Did they call the land you are on something different than what it goes by now? There are websites like https://native-land.ca that have mapped all this out—how helpful!

Once you have this all figured out, add the relevant names to the acknowledgment below. If you have a meeting with fellow activists or a date with your coven, make time for this statement at the beginning.

We honor and acknowledge the land we stand on. This is occupied territory that was once called **(NAME)** and is home to **(TRIBE/NATION)**. We acknowledge that this land was stolen by settlers, and that the mistreatment of its first people continues to this day. While we live in a world that settlers created, we promise to work on building a better world with the help and leadership of this land's original inhabitants. We honor this land and thank you for the many gifts you give us each day. Thank you for allowing us to fight on, with and for you.

✳ ✳ ✳

A CLEANSING RITUAL

I promised you a more in-depth cleansing ritual in chapter 2 and now I'm delivering!

As I said all those many pages ago, cleansing can be about wiping off spiritual gunk, but it can also be about helping further spiritual transformation. Here, I'm going to give you ways to do both.

In the spirit of the previous exercise, here are some not-sage-y, not-palo santo-y ways to remove the spiritual stuff you don't want sticking around anymore:

Try burning:

℃ Cedar

℃ Mugwort*

℃ Frankincense

℃ Pine resin

℃ Rosemary

Try washing with:

℃ Rue

℃ Hyssop

℃ Rosemary

℃ Angelica root

℃ Pine tar

For a transformative form of cleansing, do the following:

• Recognize that a bad thing happened. Maybe you hurt someone, or maybe you were hurt by someone. Much as that sucks, you are acknowledging it, which is the first step in moving past it!

• Knowing what bad thing happened, sit for a moment and think of

---

* But not if you're pregnant!

how to transform it. You can't go back and unmake it, so instead, what are you learning from it? This may take more than one sitting to uncover and might be done best with some tarot cards or a therapist—or both!

- Once you've got the Bad Thing nailed down, as well as the Good Lesson you want to turn it into, get your cleansing supplies together.
- Steep the herbs you will be using in water, if you are going to be using water, or get the burnable herbs and an object to burn them on like a shell or plate.
- Wash yourself first. Take a shower or bath.
- While you are still naked, do your spiritual cleansing. Stay in the shower or tub if you are using water.
- Keep in mind the Bad Thing you are washing away, and wash down your body. Starting with your head, wash or swipe the smoke downward in a counterclockwise direction.
- When this feels sufficiently wiped away, think about the Good Lesson you are trying to cultivate. Wipe up your body, now in a clockwise direction, until you feel this start to seep into you.

Cleansing, like all magic, is rarely a one-and-done sort of deal. Depending on what you are trying to transform and move past, this might take some time, but keep at it! We are all works in progress, and magic can help us with that progress! This particular approach doesn't have to be your go-to in all matters of cleansing, but give it a try and see how it feels when you are dealing with hurts that go a bit beneath the skin.

✳ ✳ ✳

MAKING AND WORKING WITH SPIRIT ALLIES

Witches throughout time have worked with spirits to help them cast spells, cure diseases, and defend themselves against enemies. Well, we've got plenty of enemies out there now, so I think it's about time we start making allies!

- Figure out the spirit you want to talk to and why. The good thing is you can talk to anything for any reason, but maybe try this out on smaller stuff before your fly across the country and climb a mountain to ask it for world peace.
- Tell the place/object/spirit what your intentions are and what you want out of a relationship. Are you looking for a new friend or do you have a direct action coming up and you need to make sure the conditions will be right for it? What you are asking for is going to determine what you do in the next bit.
- Make an appropriate offering. This can go from a glass of water and some incense smoke to a full bottle of booze and a home-cooked meal. I leave this bit up to your discretion—just remember not to litter and not to put yourself into debt because of this step.
- Once you've made your offering, ask for a concrete sign it's been accepted. This sign can be gleaned through your doing divination or can come in the form of birdcalls, wind gusts, or other natural phenomena. Go to the Talking to Land Spirits exercise (see page 136) for more info on what a personal language around this might look like.

- If you don't get a sign or you get a bad one, don't worry, but you probably shouldn't move ahead with your magical plans. This goes for plans big and small. Are you asking to pick an herb to use in a charm and your offering isn't received? Don't do it. Are you asking permission to build a highway and the spirits tell you no? Ditto.
- If you get the go-ahead, push on! Do your magic, and remember to say thank you somehow when the spirits grant your request. How you thank them I also leave up to you.

You'll notice that this set of instructions is nonspecific, but that's intentional. What spirits you talk to, the reasons you talk to them, what offerings you can make, and how you communicate are going to depend on your culture, practice, financial situation, and location.

Here's one recommendation about offerings, though. Some water and a loaf of bread might cut it for a one-and-done situation with a spirit. You know, if you need to get some rent money together and fast, so come on spirits let's do this thing! But for spirits you want a long-term, deep relationship with, a little bit more is the way to go. Whatever spirits you end up working with, be they of place, rock, plant, animal, or idea, there is a good chance that they are now threatened by one of the many isms running rampant in our world. Think long and deeply about how your activism can help them, and let this be your offering. What you are able to give will obviously vary, and spirits know this, but just showing up and working on their behalf is the best way to make allies in this world or any other.

✳ ✳ ✳

REINVENTING THE WHEEL OF THE YEAR

I love the Wheel of the Year. I really, really do. But some people? Boy, they really don't gel with it, and this is totally understandable. I grew up in a place where the Wheel of the Year actually made sense. The town I grew up in was tiny—like two thousand people, two stoplights tiny. But it was also a tourist town, so that meant that in the winter about two or three stores were open and everything else was literally dead, and in the summer everything was open, alive, and there were people *everywhere*. The spokes on the wheel matched up perfectly with my lived experience. In fact, it was so perfectly natural it was one of the things that first pulled me to witchcraft. It just made *sense*.

There's a good chance the classic wheel makes not a lick of sense to you. Maybe you live somewhere where it's always warm and sunny, and this idea of "the return of the light" is laughable. Maybe you live "down unda," and the wheel is flipped on its head. Maybe, like a good chunk of people, you live in a place with four seasons and solstices where they're "supposed to be," but you feel utterly disconnected from what they actually mean. And maybe on top of all that, the seasons where you live have been thrown off by, I don't know, climate change?

What all this boils down to is that having a calendar based in natural cycles and both material and spiritual conditions makes sense, but that time and calendars aren't a one-size-fits-all thing. In this exercise I'm going to take you through how "the witch's calendar" is traditionally supposed to work, and if it doesn't line up for you, I'm going to teach you how to remix it to better match the conditions of your life.

SAMHAIN (October 31)

Isn't it great when Halloween is also your New Year's Eve? The best holiday, no questions asked, kicks off the traditional Wheel of the Year with a bang. The last of the old-time harvest festivals, from here the dead lay claim over the land until six months later on Beltane. It's a day for honoring the dead and dressing up to harass your neighbors for candy.

YULE (Winter Solstice)

This is the longest night of the year. If winter is the dead overtaking the earth, Yule is the day they consume it completely. Don't worry though, because after this, the light only grows until six months later, on the summer solstice. It's a good day for divination and communing with spooky, dark entities.

IMBOLC (February 2)

You can feel spring is just around the corner, can't you? The days are getting longer again, and people are ready to be done with all the dark moodiness they've been carrying around. This is actually when most witch trials happened back in the day, because hey, after a long winter you may want to kill that weird neighbor of yours. Imbolc's message is "have hope." This is the final push, your second wind before the return of spring!

OSTARA (Spring Equinox)

Day and night are equal now until the scales tip and light triumphs! The dead have not all gone back to underworld, but the spirits of life and growing things are finally starting to get their groove back. Expect longer days and shorter nights for six months until the autumnal equinox. It's a good day for starting new things and planting yourself into good soil.

BELTANE (May 1)

Beltane is Halloween in reverse. Instead of the dead laying claim to the earth, now the spirits of life get to have their way for six months. Flowers are waving their sex organs around for all to see (and some people are too). This is the difference between a Marilyn Manson show and a Björk show (I'm a nineties kid, in case you couldn't tell)—both are days for partying and getting weird, but one is a celebration of death and the triumph of the underworld, while the other is a celebration of life and the triumph of the living earth. For our purposes in its incarnation as May Day, May 1 is also a holiday celebrated by socialists, anarchists, and lefty rabble-rousers the world over as one to fight for, and celebrate, liberation.

LITHA (Summer Solstice)

This is the longest day of the year. It's Icarus before he falls out of the sky. The gods of life are fully in the driver's seat today. It's a reminder to live while you're alive, because after today the days will grow shorter and the nights longer, until darkness takes hold once more. This is a big day for big magic—if there's a holiday for dreaming big, it's this one.

LUGHNASADH (August 1)

You feel the shadows begin to creep farther and linger longer. The trees that were fully green just weeks ago have been tinged with orange by the summer heat. Fall is on its way, and winter soon behind it. This is the first of the big harvest festivals, a time to start reaping what you have sown while the earth was in bloom.

MABON (Autumn Equinox)

The first day of fall is another day when time hangs in the balance. After this, we hop off the edge of the cliff and dive into the darkness below. This is the second harvest festival, after you have reaped your lessons from the year; how will you store them and let them sustain you through the darkness to come?

✳ ✳ ✳

Now that you know how the Wheel of the Year breaks down, here is what I want you to do if the above doesn't map well onto your life.

- Take out a calendar. If all you have is an old one or a digital one, that's fine.

- Mark on that calendar the traditional holidays that *do* make sense. Personally, even if they don't feel great for now, I really, *really* think you should at least keep the solstices and equinoxes in there since those are actual cosmic things that govern life on this planet.

- Did you keep some of them? All of them? Why or why not? What about them makes sense or doesn't make sense based on where and how you live?

- Now go through the calendar, starting in January, and explore how each month or season feels to you. Like with the land exercise, write down what sensations, colors, songs, and food they remind you of. It's okay if February only makes you think of hearts and October only makes you think of pumpkins. This is about attuning yourself to the rhythm of time within your community and environment.

- Write down any holidays that you want to add, and cut out any that don't make sense to you. Maybe you don't celebrate Christmas, or you want to add the feast day of a saint. This is about marking dates that mean something to *you* and where you live.

- Example: My new year isn't January 1 or Halloween like it's "supposed" to be for witches, because growing up, neither made sense. Halloween was the very end of "the season" and pretty much everything died after that, but that's not really a "new" year. The traditional witchy new year was just sleeping to me. So the new year I decided makes sense is the winter solstice, since that's tied to the light, and growing up our whole economy and way of life were built on the light.

- After you've added and subtracted special days that make sense to you and move your year along, take a step back—what does it look like? Is it a neat circle, or are some times of the year fuller than others? How does this echo the rhythms of the seasons where you live?

Calendars give depth perception to time. They help us orient ourselves to our environment and ground us in rhythms that keep us from being alienated. Whatever your Wheel of the Year looks like at the end of this exercise, make sure it makes you feel grounded and connected.

ACKNOWLEDGMENTS

Who do you thank for helping you write your first book? In many ways I feel like I should be thanking everyone I have met up until this point, good and bad, for forming me into the person who could craft this. If you have touched my life, even briefly, you are to thank for the work you hold in your hands.

There are, however, some people in particular I want to thank, without whom this book could never have come into being.

To the trees on which this book is printed, I pray my work is worthy of your sacrifice.

Ancestors, thank you for being the wave that brought me to the shore I am on.

Shannon Connors Fabricant, you were the best editor I could have asked for on this project. Thank you for reaching out and trusting me with this work, and for being midwife to my first baby. I quite literally could never have done this without you.

To everyone at Running Press, thank you for your support throughout the writing of this book. You made my first true literary project a delightful and easy process every step of the way.

Andy, Cal, and everyone behind the Trans Rite of Ancestor Elevation, thank you so much for letting me share your work and magic. Thank you also for working with me to make the version of it printed in this book the best it could be. May you never thirst.

Alex Avalos, thank you for introducing me to the Zapatistas so long ago, and for being a friend to me, especially when I felt like I had none.

To Tim McCarthy, who passed away just before I got this book deal. I hope you're raising hell in heaven.

Kelly McClure and Blossom Johnson, our trip to Standing Rock forever changed my life, and I couldn't have asked for better people to go on that journey with than both of you.

Kim Fraczek of the Sane Energy Project, thank you for being the first person to teach me power mapping. I hope the world is as transformed by your wisdom and fire as I continue to be.

Silvia Federici, your writing has been a deep inspiration to me for years now, and meeting you was like meeting a teacher I had studied under for years but never really known.

Monica Hunken, you are the greatest direct action trainer in the world, and the best person I could have shared my first arrest with. You've taught me to think deeply about what freedom means, and what we should do with it while we have it.

Callie Beusman, thank you for being a wonderful first editor to me early in my career, and for helping me so much when I was essentially an infant in the terrifying world of digital media.

To all my friends and comrades in the Democratic Socialists of America, New York City Chapter, EcoSocialist Working Group, you bear the burden of the longest activist group name in history with grace. More than that, you all inspire me every day to challenge myself, grow, and constantly expand my horizons of political possibilities. Because of you all, I truly believe a better world is possible.

To Catland, and the New York occult community. I didn't feel like I really had a home before you.

Ani Simon Kennedy, you were the first person to trust me to tell my story on camera. You and the folks of *Teen Vogue* launched my career, and I'll be forever thankful.

And finally, to my friends who stuck by me when things were so, so difficult, thank you for showing me what the word family means.

INDEX